No Breakup Can Break You:
The Definitive Recovery Guide for Men

D1727510

NICK DAWSON

CONTENTS

DISCLAIMER

This book is based on personal opinion, experience, and relatable research. The author, however, is not a licensed therapist, and nothing within should be taken as professional advice. Always consult a professional before making any medical, legal or business decisions.

FORWARD

You just cracked open 98-pages of certified heartbreak repellent. No, no. Don't go rubbing it up and down your body. My name's on this thing, and that would just be awkward for the both of us.

Instead, I want you to get ready to put this terrible, miserable, god-awful breakup behind you. Here's the good news: right now, you're closer to getting over this breakup than you probably realize. Even if it feels like you just took a spinning back kick right to your soul. Even if it feels like your happiness just got punted into a different dimension. Truth be told, you're well on your way to getting over this breakup and getting on with your life. How can I be so sure? Two reasons: first off, if you're reading this book right now, that means you either did some seriously wild misclicking while searching for crockpot recipes, or more likely, you've been dealing with a breakup, stumbled across this book, and picked it up for the specific purpose of getting over your ex and getting on with your life. What that tells me is that you're already coming to terms with what happened in your relationship. You're not ignoring the situation, pretending everything's fine, trying to win your ex back, or waiting around for that one phone call that will fix everything. No, by picking this book up, you've proven that you're not in denial about this whole thing, and that means you're way ahead of the game already.

Secondly, if you're reading this book right now, that means you haven't decided to simply crawl into bed, curse the world, and wait for the heat death of the universe either. You haven't given in to apathy. Sure, you may be in bed. Sure, you may be cursing the world, but just by reading these first few paragraphs, you're proving that you're ready and willing to get to work. As countless philosophers and fortune cookies have said before me, "every journey begins with a single step." And here you are, taking the first step right this second.

So, how do I know you can get through this? Because you've already dodged two of the biggest pitfalls. You're not in denial, which means you're ready to face this breakup head on. Plus, you've put apathy on the back burner for the time being and taken your first steps to getting your life back on track. You're exactly where you need to be to start this recovery, and with this book as your wingman, not only will you send your heartbreak packing, there's a good chance you'll become a better man by the time we're done. To put it simply, this breakup sure as hell isn't going to break you. So, let's get to it...

CHAPTER 1
- The Two Hurdles of Heartbreak -

Remember that scene in the movie *Alien* when everyone was enjoying a nice dinner, and then all of a sudden, the ugliest ferret you've ever seen burst out of that one guy's chest? Movie fact: If you listen very carefully, you can actually hear him say, "This is still better than my last breakup!" That's because breaking up doesn't just hurt. It hits you at the center of your being and makes you question everything you are and everything you've ever done. It can shatter your confidence and leave you utterly miserable. It can put your entire life on pause, and make you seriously consider finding a cave in the woods, switching on Hermit-mode, and staying there until the robots rise up.

Of course, while living in a literal man-cave does have a certain appeal, it probably wouldn't do you much good in the breakup department. Truth is, to get over this breakup, there's really only two things you need to do: you have to break your biological addiction to your ex and you have to mentally move on from the relationship. That's it. Just two things, and that's exactly what we'll cover in the coming chapters.

"But wait!" You shout to no one in particular. "According to my *Handbook of Male Stereotypes,* the only thing a guy needs to do after a breakup is…

Step 1: Apply beer directly to the wound
Step 2: Drop a mortgage payment on the nearest stripper
Step 3: Talk to literally anyone about their transmission

And Step 4: Oh my god, dude, it's been like two days. Get over it already."

First off, please burn that book and bury the ashes. Secondly, this is the reason why I wanted to write this guide. When I went through my breakup, there wasn't much help out there for guys. Despite there being scientific research that breakups are harder for men than they are for women,[1] the world pretty much told me to drink more beer, hang out with more strippers, and just walk it off already. Unfortunately, that wasn't exactly the breakup breakthrough I was looking for. Fact is, there are some things you can't walk off. A broken leg, for example. Or in this case, a broken heart. Instead of pretending everything's fine and secretly hoping to feel better one day, the best thing you can do right now is face your breakup head on and start working your way through it.

Of course, getting over a breakup isn't the kind of thing you can knock out over lunch. It's going to take time and it's going to take work, but it doesn't have to be as bad as many people will tell you. I've often heard that no matter how long you've been in a relationship, it'll take half that time to get over its breakup. For example, if you were together six years, it'll take you three years to recover. Ten years? Then you're looking at five years of waiting.

With all due respect to the burgeoning field of Romantic Mathematics – to hell with all that. No one has that kind of time lying around. Instead of spending years waiting to suddenly be cured, we're going to focus on the two most important tasks at hand: breaking your biological addiction and getting you to mentally move on. Of course, in order to tackle those two tasks, there are two big hurdles standing in your way. These are the two reasons you feel the way you do right now. These are the two reasons you can't simply let go and move on. Let's take a look at each of them…

Hurdle #1: The Biological Imperative

Remember how cool your brain was back when you were dating? It was always coming up with witty things to say, and remembering anniversaries, and keeping your heart beating and whatnot. Despite how dependable it's been in the past, after a breakup, it's going to turn on you like you just slapped its grandmother in the mouth. It's going to pull a complete 180 and go out of its way to purposefully make you feel terrible. It's going to ruin your sleep and your appetite. It's going to make you feel guilty and lonely and take you on one hell of an emotional rollercoaster ride. Basically, it's going to turn into four pounds of pure, concentrated bastard, but to its credit, it's only doing what it thinks is best for you.

Despite our mighty civilizations and impressive technology, human beings are still animals, and we all have very biologically ingrained urges to help us survive. Take hunger for example. When your blood sugar is low, or your stomach is empty, your body releases specific hormones that signal your brain to create a very real and very uncomfortable sensation of hunger. Now we all know that hunger can be a very unpleasant feeling, but in reality, it has to be. It has to motivate you to find food. It has to spur you into action.

It has to be so unpleasant that hundreds of thousands of years ago our ancestors would leave their warm fires, head into the unknown, and risk their lives to bring home dinner.

Hunger hurts, but your primal brain is a very firm believer in tough love. It's really only concerned with two things: preservation and procreation. It's not designed to take your personal comfort level into account. If it did - if it said, "sure thing, buddy, let's take the day off. We can always go hunting next week" - our species would have gone extinct a long, long time ago. After all, if hunger didn't hurt, you might not eat enough. You might get weaker. You might end up starving. And that's not a risk your brain is willing to take. That's why it has to take control and motivate you the best it can — even if it's painful.

During a breakup, your brain is going to do the same exact thing, and it's not going to pull any punches. It's going to use various neurotransmitters to create powerful sensations of misery, longing and pain in order to provoke you to get back together with your ex. These sensations are so bad that going through a breakup produces the same brain patterns as if you were going through cocaine withdrawals.[2] These feelings are powerful. They are terrible. But it's important to remember that they are also natural. Despite how bad you are feeling right now, your brain is simply doing what it thinks is best for you and the species as a whole. After all, we didn't always live in huge cities and drive cars and have supermarkets.

Way, way back in Paleolithic times, the brains of our ancient ancestors whipped up their chemical combinations to make sure people kept looking for food, that they formed tribes for safety, and that they reproduced often. While this system obviously worked great for mankind way back when, it hasn't received a software update in a few million years. That's why, today, this primal part of your brain is completely out of its element when it comes to dating. It doesn't understand breakups because there were no breakups back in prehistoric times. Getting stepped on by a mammoth? There's your breakup. Frankly, tribes were too small and the world was too dangerous to handle big romantic conflict. Ug-Ug the Cavegirl wouldn't just wake up one day, say she's tired of being in a relationship, flip off the entire tribe, and walk off into the woods to get eaten by a giant snake. That wouldn't be good for the tribe or the entire species (great for the snake though). And that's why we're hardwired to discourage those sorts of things from happening. That's why we feel fear. That's why we get lonely. That's why we naturally want to keep relationships and build communities. It's for our own personal survival and the survival of our species as a whole.

Of course, our newly-found intellect does give us the power to override some of these imperatives. We can go on diets, despite how hungry we get. We can face our fears, even if we are terrified. And we can break up, even if we are programmed to pair bond. Unfortunately, if the breakup came suddenly, if you haven't had time to mentally break those bonds, the more difficult and more painful things are going to be. If you were strongly pair-bonded when the relationship came to an end, your brain is going to lose its damn mind, so to speak. It's going to see this event as a huge threat to its biological imperatives of reproduction, safety, and community, and it's going to do its damnedest to drive you and your ex back together.

This is why most people who get broken up with have a nearly uncontrollable urge to contact and be near their ex. They'll call, text, email, cyberstalk, send flowers, and drop by unannounced. And while this chemically-motivated smothering technique is guaranteed to fail, your primal brain simply doesn't know any better. It has zero game when it comes to the modern world. Like the first zookeeper who got ahold of two pandas, it simply assumes that if it can get you and your ex in the same room together, everything will just work itself out. Romance will blossom, you'll start cranking out babies left and right, and the species will be saved. That's how things worked in the land before time, but in today's world, you simply have to put up with your brain's old-fashioned way of doing things. At least, for a time.

Despite how powerful and painful these emotions feel right now, the biggest takeaway here is to remember that these feelings are not a cosmic sign that you and your ex were destined to be together, that she is the only one for you, or that you'll never be happy again. I know you probably feel terrible right now. Beyond terrible. But trust me, these emotions will eventually dull and fade. All this misery is just your brain trying to keep the status oh so quo, but it will eventually give up. You will get through this, and to help, we're going to throw an all-out intervention for your ex-addiction and speed you to recovery.

Of course, while biology plays a huge role in every breakup, your conscious, thinking mind is also going to be reeling from a bruised ego, rejection, and feelings of shame and guilt. This is what our second hurdle is all about, and we're going to take good care of this one as well.

Hurdle #2: Backward Thinking

While your biological imperative works at the unconscious level to influence your mood and behavior, your waking, conscious mind is going to have a whole lot to say about this breakup as well. Again, this is not entirely your brain's fault. It's simply doing what it's designed to do. Your conscious mind is a problem-solver, and this breakup is on the very top of its To-Solve list. It's going to want to get all Sherlock Holmesy on this thing, take a magnifying glass to your entire relationship, dig up the clues, and try to find logic in something that's many times illogical. It'll want to figure out where it all went wrong, if you can still fix things, why you couldn't make it work, and the only way it can do that is by thinking things through.

Unless you have the mental fortitude of an 80-year-old Tibetan monk, however, you're going to find yourself dealing with a variety of negative and irrational thoughts during this process. This is what I refer to as Backward Thinking. These kinds of thoughts don't help with your recovery. They don't empower you or motivate you to push ahead. They simply sap your resolve and drag you backwards. Here are a few examples that might be making a cameo appearance in your head...

1. Self-blaming. This is one of the big traps that

many guys fall into. No matter what you did in the relationship, you might start to think that this breakup was entirely your fault. All that blame will lead to feelings of guilt, and that guilt will lead to feeling miserable. And that's no way to move ahead. Truth is, everyone makes mitsakes. You made some. Your ex made some. Every person who's ever been in a relationship has made some. You can either think of them as important lessons that will make you an even better partner in the future, or you can let that guilt rob you of any motivation to move ahead. Personally, I say we stick with the former. As it turns out, no person in history has ever felt so guilty that they were instantly flung back in time to fix their mistakes. Guilt is not a DeLorean. It won't take you back in time. It'll just waste the time you have.

2. The Should Have's. This is self-blaming's scrappy little sidekick. And by sidekick, I mean it will happily kick you while you're down, right in the side. The Should Have's refer to all the things you believe you should have done during the relationship, or especially at the very end, that could have stopped the breakup from happening.

"I should have been more loving."
"I should have been less clingy."
"I should have told her how I really felt."
"I should have kept my mouth shut."
"I should have given her everything."
"I should have stopped spoiling her."

No matter what you did right, after a breakup, you'll think you did everything wrong. And that's confidence kryptonite. Just as guilt cannot change the past, neither will regret. The best you can do is learn from your mistakes. If you don't believe me, just imagine that you could go back and talk to your former self, the one still in the relationship. Imagine what you would say to him. You'd tell him how to avoid every mistake. You'd guide him through every pitfall. You'd make up graphs and diagrams and charts explaining exactly what to do and what not do. You could talk to him for hours and hours about this breakup, right? And you know what that tells me? You've learned a ton from this breakup already. Just think how far you've come from that guy just a few weeks or months ago. Think how much more you know now. The truth is, people can only learn so much from their successes, but they can learn life-changing things from their mistakes. And this breakup, no matter how painful, has already taught you amazingly valuable things. Instead of worrying about what you should have done in the past, take heart that you now know what to do in the future.

3. The Fear Mentality. These thoughts love to hitch a ride on the blame train. You'll be beating yourself up about some mistake in the past, and suddenly you're taking an unscheduled trip to Neverland...

"I'm never going to find someone as smart/pretty/funny as she was."

"I'm never going to be happy again."

"I'm never going to be able to trust someone."

"I'm never going to get through this."

"I'm never going to have to work again because I'm a powerful psychic, and I know all the sports scores for the next hundred years."

Okay, you're not a psychic, and you don't know

what's going to happen in the future. With these kinds of thoughts, however, you are shaping the future – and not in a good way. Instead of seeing the infinite potential ahead of you, you become afraid that you've ruined things. That you're not good enough. That your best times are behind you. That you'll never find happiness again. This is the fear mentality at its worst, and just for the record, it's completely wrong. You will be happy again. You will find someone just as great, or even better for you. You will do amazing things if you want to. But first, you have to break through all these backward thoughts and start moving ahead. In the next chapter, we'll discuss how to get your thoughts, fears and worries under control. By the time we're done, your fears will be having nightmares about you.

So How Do I Know What the Hell I'm Talking About?

I'll be upfront with you. I'm not a therapist and I don't even play one on TV. I'm just a guy who went through a breakup so bad its theme song could go platinum on the country music charts. In the end, I lost my wife, my house, my dog, a third of my life savings, and for a time, my happiness.

To give you the short and sweet of it, I met an amazing girl in my last year of college, and after eight great years together, we got married. Some people asked me why I waited so long to propose, but basically, I didn't want to become another divorce statistic. I had seen so many divorces in my life that I wanted to make absolutely, positively sure that when I got married, it was one and done.

The wedding itself was spectacular. In front of our friends and family, we dedicated our lives to each other. From there, cake led to dancing. Dancing led to the honeymoon. The honeymoon led to married life. And that led to problems. Unfortunately, only two months after our wedding, her attitude suddenly turned sharp and cold towards me. It was like day and night. She started staying out late with her friends and going out of her way to avoid being with me. Eight weeks beforehand, she had wanted to spend the rest of her life with me. Now she couldn't bear spending an entire day. I could hear it in her voice. I could see it in the way she looked at me. I was losing her for some reason, and that thought crushed me.

I pleaded with her to tell me what had happened. What had I done wrong? What can I do to fix it? Why was she pulling away from me? I would have done anything. After weeks of desperate questioning, she finally came clean. During one of those late nights out, a coworker had professed his love for her, and now she wasn't so sure about me anymore. She told me that this guy understood her better. They had more things in common. They were better suited for each other. And those were hard things to hear from the woman you wanted to grow old with.

Three months after she said "I do," she said "I'm done," and left in the middle of the night. I moved out of our place soon after that, and besides a quick divorce signing, I haven't seen her since. I'd like to think that, after spending eight years together, even M. Night Shyamalan couldn't have come up with a better twist ending than that. Even if we both turned out to be ghosts.

Now, I'm not trying to out breakup-story anyone here. Believe me. Despite how bad it was, even my lawyer told me that I got off lucky, and chances are that your breakup is far worse than mine. Still, I wanted you to know that I've been there. I'm on a first-name basis with all those terrible emotions you're feeling right now, and I know how brutal they can be.

So, how did I get through it? After my divorce, I needed a place to stay pretty much immediately and since all my money was tied up, I did what every single guy dreams of doing when he's about to turn 30. I moved into a tiny apartment in the middle of Chinatown with my *mom*. If you just cringed reading that, so did I. Now, while I admit being surrounded by five different dim sum restaurants was fairly glorious, at the emotional level, I was still devastated. For about a month, I just zombied-out, and not like one of those cool, modern-day zombies who can run a five-minute mile and seem like they have their lives all figured out either. I was definitely one of those slow, groany zombies from the 1950s that you could sidestep in your sleep. I pretty much stumbled from place to place, cold, detached, and slightly drooling. By that point, I was all kinds of bitter, and ten kinds of miserable, and basically, you wouldn't have wanted me at your birthday party.

From there, I wish I could tell you that I ended up backpacking through Europe and ultimately discovered the truth behind love, life and happiness. But to be honest, I was stuck in Chinatown, and the only thing I wanted months after my divorce was to stop feeling like crap for a few minutes. That was my driving force: is there any way to feel slightly less terrible at this point? Sure, it wasn't the sexiest of goals, but it gave me a place to start. Thing is, I wanted to get better. I wanted to be happy again. And I wanted it to happen as soon as possible. I felt like I had wasted so much of my past that I didn't want to waste another second of my future. And so, I started looking for answers. I figured, if there was something out there that could help me, I was going to find it and wring every little drop of relief out of it I could. To start, I read all the breakup books I could find, even though they were all written specifically for women. I admit, it was a little strange being told over and over again that I was a stone-cold fox who didn't need a man to be happy, but hey, I rolled with it. After that, I spent hours and hours on breakup forums reading people's stories and other people's suggestions. I dove into psychology journals to get a more scientific perspective on breakups, relationships and rejection. I even went to a therapist for a few months to get a professional opinion. Whatever it took, I was down, and eventually, I found things that made a real difference. Some were obvious. Some were a little strange. Some I'll use for the rest of my life.

I wasn't planning on writing a book, of course. I just wanted to feel better, and eventually I really did. With everything I learned though, I occasionally went back to those breakup forums and offered my own advice. I liked being able to return the favor. On one occasion, however, one of my posts got pretty popular and someone even replied by saying, "Wow, you should really write a book." Of course, with the internet being what it is, there's a good chance that guy was being sarcastic, but that was a risk I decided to take. And so, a couple days after that reply, I started outlining this book, and now, you're reading what it came to be.

I've taken all the best techniques, all the things I wish I knew back then, and put them into this book. It's packed with everything you need to know to get over your ex, and also, how to start working towards an even better future.

After all, when the dust settled, and my breakup was behind me, I was stronger, more focused and happier than I had ever been before. Looking back now, my breakup was a blessing, and I'm confident that you will feel the same way, someday, too. And this book will help you along the way. Remember, even the stars fall down sometimes. You may be down and out right now, but that will just make your rise all the sweeter. The next chapters will guide you onward and upward, and when you look back, and see how far you've come, you'll truly be amazed. You can get through this, and if you really commit yourself, if you really focus, you can make this breakup the best thing that's ever happened to you. It's all up to you.

CHAPTER 2
- What to Do Right Now -

Strap yourself in my friend because your recovery starts right here. Chapter Two contains all the techniques you need to put into action ASAP. While we will be diving into long-term strategies later on in this book, this chapter details all the things you need to start doing right now to jump-start your recovery. I personally used each of these techniques during my breakup, and I think they will work wonders for you. Sure, every relationship may be wildly different, and every breakup may have its own causes, but in the end, every recovery shares the same hurdles. Each person on the wrong-end of a breakup has to deal with their biological addiction and the cognitive effects of rejection. The techniques in this chapter work by tackling both of these issues. Use them all together and you can quiet your biological imperative, counteract all those negative chemicals you're facing, and kick those backward thoughts of yours to the curb. That's what you need right now. That's what will get you through this. And that's just what we aim to do…

Say Yes to No Contact

No Contact is the definitive, go-to, time-tested, mother-approved strategy for pretty much any breakup, and if you broke up recently, you're going to most likely hate it. Like the name implies, no contact means stopping all communication with your ex, whether that means calling, texting, emailing, Facebooking,

Tweeting, or whatever. It especially means no face-to-face contact, which your biological imperative is not going to be happy about one bit. Instead of no contact right now, your brain wants mo' contact. It wants you to be near her. It wants you to call her. It wants you to sleep on the hood of her car just so you can say hi to her in the morning (Disclaimer: Don't do this). Even though every fiber in your being is telling you to be near her, the best thing you can do is actually cut all contact. It doesn't have to be forever. It doesn't have to be rude or hurtful. It's just has to happen.

So why does it work so well? Right now, your primal brain is making you feel terrible, because during our evolution, having a partner was better for you and the survival of the species. But what if you and your ex got separated and it was impossible to ever see her again? What if she had to travel far away and there was absolutely no chance of ever getting back together? Would your primal brain want you to suffer forever? Would making you feel miserable be good for you or the survival of the species in the long run? That's a no.

By starting no contact, and sticking with it, you'll slowly convince your brain that reconciliation is an impossibility. Over time, it'll begin to realize that no matter how many pain chemicals it throws at you, you're not getting back together. And because it won't risk all future relationships for an impossible one, it will eventually give up. It will decide that preparing for a new partner is much more productive than trying to reconcile with an old one that's completely out of reach. Before it gets this message though, it's going to test you. It wants to make absolutely sure that this relationship is not going to happen, and I won't sugarcoat it, the first month will be tough. You'll feel extremely lonely. She'll be on your mind constantly. You'll try to convince yourself that sending her one or two texts couldn't hurt, but you have to stay strong. If you keep talking to her and seeing her, your brain will keep cranking out those bad chemicals because it knows she's nearby.

If you cut all contact, however, slowly but surely your brain will get the hint that it's over. You'll start thinking about her less and start thinking about your future more. You'll begin to feel better. Much better. You might get a desperate need to contact her every now and again, but you'll learn to control it. You'll realize that you are stronger than your emotions. That you have a willpower worth bragging about. And that you can overcome great obstacles, if you put your mind to it. And one unassuming day, you'll find yourself laughing and smiling and having a great time, and she won't be there. And you'll realize that she doesn't have to be. She wasn't the key to your happiness after all. It was simply hidden away, and you just had to find it again.

Before you can say hello to this bright future though, you have to say goodbye to your ex. At least for a time. If she has a habit of contacting you still, gather your thoughts and then send her a text or an email. Tell her that you'd appreciate some time and space. Tell her that she shouldn't contact you anymore. That means no phone calls, texts, IMs, emails, or anything. Tell her that you're not trying to be petty or spiteful. Tell her that this is just what you need right now. It's for the best. Then hit send, and finally, congratulate yourself. It's not easy to say goodbye, even if it's only for a short time, but it's worth it.

From there, we can jump to Phase Two. At its heart, no contact isn't exclusively about cutting communication. It's about reducing all those daily reminders of your ex as well. If you keep seeing her, even in photos, that will only slow your recovery. As they say, "out of sight, out of mind," and so we've got some work to do...

o It's time to clean house. Grab all those pictures, vacation souvenirs, cards, mementos, and toss them in a box. You don't have to get rid of them, you just need to get them out of your sight.

o If you two frequent the same social media sites, either block her or unfriend her. You don't need all those updates thrown in your face on a daily basis. You may also want to block her close friends and family, if she will appear in a lot of their posts.

o Do you have pictures of her on your phone, tablet and computer? Gather them all up and put them in a folder away from your prying eyes.

There will still be a ton of things that will remind you of her, and that's okay. These small steps will help, and the simple act of getting up, taking action, and being in control of your breakup for once will make you feel better. It's all part of the cleansing process. Or as I call it, the EX-foliation Process. (don't worry, I don't actually call it that).

So, you know why you should start No Contact, and you know how to get it done, but you might still have reservations. If you're anything like I was, you've probably already come up with a half dozen reasons why No Contact can wait. I understand. I know how tough it is to walk away from a person you've shared your life with, but it's not about her anymore, it's about you. And this is the quickest way for you to get back on your feet. If you're still having reservations, allow me to address a few of the most common concerns, one by one...

"What if she wants to get back together? If I don't talk to her, she will think I'm not interested anymore."

This is the question that kept me texting. What if she changes her mind? What if she realizes she's made a mistake? I have to stay on her mind, right? Here's the thing: you can't argue your way into anyone's heart. There's nothing you can say, that you haven't said already, that will make her change her mind. Love is a feeling. An emotion. And you can't argue it into submission. In fact, if you're feeling desperate, nervous and clingy right now, you'll only push her further away. By cutting communication, however, she will finally see what it's like to be without you. If you're always there for her, if you keep showering her with attention, she will end up taking you for granted. Things only become valuable when they are in limited supply, so why make yourself so available?

Of course, you should never waste time hoping and waiting for a reconciliation. That will only keep you stuck in the past, but rest assured, if reconciliation is possible, no contact will not ruin your chances. By now, she knows how you feel, and if she happens to have a change of heart, she will let you know. No Contact isn't going to stop her. They say true love conquers all, and that includes a block on Facebook. In the end, you're not risking your reconciliation by starting No Contact. You're only risking a lot more time and heartbreak by postponing it.

"She's an amazing person, and I still want to be friends with her."

I thought about trying to be friends with my ex, but in all honesty, I would have just used that friendship to try and win her back. I would have tried to prove myself every time we met. I would have been phony and manipulative and that's not how a friendship should be. If you truly want to be friends with your ex, give yourself some time. You need to remove the romance first or the friendship will become forced and strained, and eventually, it will fail. And that won't be pretty.

You also have to ask yourself if you're really capable of being her friend and dealing with everything that comes with that. Being a real friend means never expecting more from the relationship. It means stepping aside when she finds someone new. It means being open and trustworthy and honest. If you're only being her friend to try and win her back, that's not a real friendship, and that's not fair to either of you.

Sure, I've seen lovers become good friends, and things have worked out just fine, but it's rare and it's not for everyone. Take some time, and after the romance has faded away, revisit the idea with a clear head. If your ex really is a good friend, she will understand what you're going through and give you all the space you need.

"I need to know why this happened. I need closure."

During your breakup conversation, I'm sure you asked "why?" You probably asked it many times. If she was able to give you some explanation, all you can do is accept what she said and maybe learn something from it. There's no need to argue against her reasons or keep asking for clarification. I know you want to prove her wrong, and explain your side of the story, but things don't work like that. It isn't about being right or wrong now. You can't disprove her complaints and save the relationship. She made her decision, and you have to accept that.

If her reasons don't seem compelling, or if she couldn't give you a reason at all, try not to be upset or angry. The simple truth is that she most likely doesn't understand why her feelings changed either. Emotions, especially love, don't always make sense. There is no formula for falling in love. Some guys do everything right, and their women leave. Some men do everything wrong, and their women stay. There are thousands of uncontrollable factors at play in every relationship, and if her feelings faded, that's simply how your particular relationship played out. Breaking up, in that case, is actually for the best.

If her feelings faded, for one reason or another, isn't it better that you find out now instead of spending years and years with someone who didn't really love you? Would you really want to be with someone who only stayed because she was afraid to leave? Maybe right now you're saying, "Yes, yes. I don't care. I just want her back." But be honest with yourself, you don't want that. You don't want to be in a one-sided relationship where you give 100% and she gives zero. You will only end up miserable and end up feeling far worse than you do now. You deserve to be with someone who's ready to fight for your relationship, who loves you to the brink, and that you can love in return. That's a relationship worth having, and that's what you are now free to find.

"We work together, and I have to see her every day."

There may be circumstances where no contact is a no-go. You work at the same place, have children, or still live together. That's going to make things trickier but not impossible. If you can't go No Contact, focus on Low Contact instead. Just like a limbo contest, the lower you can go, the better. After all, the more you see her, the longer it will take your brain to understand that the relationship is over. To get around this, try to downgrade any necessary communication. Instead of seeing her face-to-face, send her an email. Instead of calling her up, send her a text. Try your best to limit these interactions as well. If you do have to see her in person, keep it professional. Ditch the chit-chat. Don't bring up the relationship. And keep it brief.

If you're worried about coming off as rude or hurtful, let her know the game plan. Send her an email or text explaining that you will be there for her, when it's necessary, but you're going to limit all other interactions. You're going to keep conversations short and leave when necessary. Ask her to do the same, and not to contact you unless it is important. Once you lay down the ground rules, things will become easier, and eventually, you'll be able to separate your emotions from these interactions.

***

Whether you're going no contact or low contact, you'll probably still have to deal with plenty of urges to call or text. Maybe there's just one more thing you want to say. Maybe you want to see how she's been doing. Or maybe you saw something that you want to tell her about. Before you even touch your phone, ask yourself if it's worth it. Will this call fix anything? Is it worth breaking your track record for? It may be a relief to finally talk to her, but when she doesn't give you the attention or the answers you are looking for, you'll feel far worse.

If these call cravings hit, the best thing you can do is call someone else. Anyone else. A friend. A family member. The simple act of holding a conversation will keep your mind distracted until those urges fade away. If there's no one you can call, try to get out of the house. Go to the store. Go for a walk. Grab a bite. Just go for it. Don't sit there, staring at your phone and debating with yourself. The longer you sit around, the more you will rationalize things and the more likely you'll end up caving. Instead of letting that happen, get out of the house and take your mind off things.

At the end of the day, overcoming your biological imperative is a waiting game. But No Contact is what starts the clock. The key is to manage your symptoms, combat the negative chemicals in the meantime, and hold on strong until your brain gets the message. Day by day, week by week, you'll feel a tiny bit better, and all those bits will add up to amazing things. You'll feel more focused. More in control. And eventually, you'll go days without thinking about her. But it's all up to you. The sooner you say yes to No Contact, the sooner this can all begin.

Try Rational Rethinking

You can do amazing things with your mind. Maybe you can't bend spoons or lift semi-trucks with your thoughts, but as it turns out, you can do something almost as impressive: you can think your way to happiness. Research has proven that the right thoughts can actually shape our emotions. They can change our attitude and our outlook for the better. And in my opinion, that's way more useful than a hundred bended spoons.

During this breakup, you're going to be dealing with a metric ton of backward thoughts. Those thoughts will ruin your attitude, that attitude will lead to a variety of negative emotions, and those negative emotions will only lead to more and more backward thinking. It's a vicious cycle, and the key is to put an end to it before it even gets started.

Rational Rethinking is a very simplified version of a well-known technique called Automatic Thought Recording, which has been used in cognitive behavioral therapy sessions for decades. Despite being simplified, it's still extremely powerful and easy to use. Next time a backward thought comes out of nowhere to ruin your day, all I want you to do is calm yourself and reanalyze your thoughts rationally. Try to distance yourself from the emotions you are feeling, and then, give your thoughts a huge dose of reality. The truth about backward thoughts is that they don't give a damn about the truth. They are irrational and illogical by nature. They love to exaggerate things and make mountains out of molecules. By reanalyzing those thoughts rationally and logically, however, you can expose the exaggerations and mistruths they use to bring you down.

For example, during this breakup, you may have thought to yourself, "I screw up everything." This is a common feeling, but it's also a huge exaggeration. If you don't confront this thought head on, however, your emotions will begin to sink and you'll start to wonder if you really do screw up everything. Without a counter argument, after all, the original argument will carry a lot more weight. You'll start thinking about every mistake you've ever made, and you'll use those incidents as evidence against yourself. You'll dismiss all the great things you've done and focus entirely on the negative. Ten minutes later, this one untrue thought, "I screw up everything," will have broken your spirits and made you feel worthless. And we have to stop that from happening.

This is where Rational Rethinking comes into play. Now, let's examine your thought, "I screw up everything." This thought is blatantly false. You don't screw up everything. In fact, you succeed constantly. Did you brush your teeth today without swallowing your toothbrush? Boom. Success. Do you screw up *everything*? Absolutely not. I guarantee you've done countless great things. Have you ever made a mistake? Of course. Everyone's made mistakes in their past. Everyone's said something they regret, done something embarrassing, or hurt someone's feelings. Does that mean everyone's a failure and a screw up? No way. We are all works in progress.

Next time you think to yourself, "I screw up everything," try to rethink that thought rationally. Say to yourself, "That's a huge exaggeration. I don't screw up everything. I succeed every day. Yes, I made mistakes during my relationship, but I've learned from them, and I'll try hard to never repeat them. Every mistake I made back then will only make me better in the future."

Once you've exposed how untrue or exaggerated those backward thoughts are, they will lose their power over you. They will disappear in an instant, and more often than not, you'll end up feeling quite good afterwards too. Now, there are a few more examples below to get you started, but you will face plenty more. Stay logical. Stay rational. Stay persistent. If one thought is constantly bothering you, write your rebuttal down. These thoughts can't stand up to scrutiny, and they will eventually fade away. Whatever you do, just keep at it. Happiness might only be a few thoughts away.

Your thought: "I'm a failure."
Your response: "That's not true. The only thing that failed was my relationship. And that's okay. We just weren't right for each other, and that's nothing to be ashamed of. Nearly every single person goes through this. That doesn't mean everyone on the planet is a

failure, and it doesn't mean I'm one either."

Your thought: "I'll never be happy again."
Your response: "I'm not a psychic. How do I know I will never be happy again? If I was happy before her, I'm pretty sure I'll be happy after her. I'm just dealing with this breakup right now, but these bad feelings will eventually go away."

Your thought: "It's all my fault. I made a mistake and ruined everything."
Your response: "If I knew what would have happened, I would never have made those mistakes. I can't change the past, but I can prepare for the future. All I can do is accept the consequences and learn from them. Now that I'm wiser, chances are I can make my next relationship even better than the last."

Your thought: "She was perfect for me. I'll never find someone like her again."
Your response: "Fact is, she wasn't perfect for me, or we would still be together. Now that we're broken up, I have the opportunity to find someone who might be even better for me. Someone different. Someone who will make me happy, and who I can make happy in return."

Keep a Grateful Journal

It might sound too good to be true, but by writing three little sentences a day, you can actually change your outlook on life. Think of it as a haiku of happiness.

Every night, before you go to sleep, try writing down three great things that happened in your day or things that you are grateful for. Here's an example pulled directly from my own personal journal:

October 17th:
- I'm grateful I got to hang out with Matt and Shelley today
- I'm grateful I found a good movie to watch on my day off
- I'm grateful that ramen exists

Obviously, we're not talking Shakespeare here. These lines don't have to be fancy or clever. They can be short, sweet, and straight to the point. And the things you write about don't have to be world changing either. If you saw a friend. If you heard a good song. If you had something tasty to eat. Those are all perfect. Just by spending a little time thinking about your day and focusing on the good, instead of the bad or the ugly, you can change your whole perspective. Research is beginning to show us that happiness isn't some ethereal, unattainable goal. It's not reserved for only a lucky few. Being happy, as it turns out, is more of a skill, and it's a skill that you can get better at with practice.

Just like hitting a golf ball or making a layup, the more you do something, the better you get at it. Practice makes perfect, and that's because inside our brains, neurons are constantly connecting and rearranging so that we can learn and improve. If you go snowboarding every day, the neurons responsible for balance will join forces in your brain. They'll connect and strengthen so that you can become a better snowboarder. In the same way, by starting a Grateful Journal, your brain's positive-thinking pathways will get a much-needed workout. With a little practice, you'll start seeing the positives instead of being overwhelmed by the negatives. After all, there are always two ways to look at a problem. If you walk out and see your car has a flat tire, you might curse and scream that bad things always happen to you. It's easy to feel that way, but in almost every situation, negativity is not the answer. It won't fix your tire for you. It won't get you on the road faster. Instead, you can think to yourself, "I'm lucky this tire didn't cause an accident. And better yet, I have a spare right in the trunk. It'll only take me a few minutes to change it out." By keeping a journal, your brain will get better and better at seeing the bright side of things. It will start to become automatic. And you'll also start to appreciate all those little things that most people take for granted.

I understand it's hard to think positively when life is squeezing its lemons directly into your eyes. And that's fine. You don't have to be so cheery right now that you leave a trail of rainbows and glitter everywhere you go. I simply want you to look outside of this breakup for a change. Right now, you're wearing a huge pair of breakup goggles (they're kind of like beer goggles, but not as fun), and all you can see and focus on is what you've lost in this breakup. By spending five minutes writing in your journal, you'll begin to notice all the good things this breakup hasn't touched. You'll put this breakup in perspective and start to appreciate the little things. But persistence is key. Every night, without fail, invest those five minutes in yourself. As time goes on, you can actually get better at being happier.

Stay Social

After any breakup, it's important to call in backup. Friends. Family. Coworkers. Anybody. This is not the time to get in touch with your inner introvert. You need to be around people. You need to connect with people. And chatting with the pizza delivery guy for a few seconds every night isn't going to cut it. Humans are social creatures after all. In prehistoric times, it was extremely difficult to survive by yourself, and it was nigh impossible to raise children alone. Lone wolves didn't last long and had far fewer chances to pass on their genes. Our most successful ancestors were huge social butterflies, and that's why today, we have inherited their desire for community and their need to belong to a "tribe." This may explain why some breakups feel like a life-or-death situation, because to your primal brain, it might just be one. Losing a partner is like losing a big part of your tribe, and to your brain, that's a dangerous situation to be in. Being alone was almost a death-sentence, and so your brain is going to pummel you with feelings of loneliness and rejection in hopes that you'll reconcile with your ex and reform your tribe.

Modern relationships aren't that simple of course. We can't always get what we, or our brains, want. Instead, the best thing you can do is remind your brain that you are still connected with many other people – that you still have a tribe, even if your ex is gone. And the best way to do that is to converse and connect with other people. You need to get out of the house, strengthen old friendships and create brand new ones. At least once a week, or more if possible, try to do something social. Grab some dinner. Hit the basketball courts. Simply hang out and relax. Whatever you're into, just try to get some people involved. By being around friends and family, your brain will slowly get the message that everything's gonna be alright. You haven't been kicked out of your tribe and forced into exile. Your tribe just went through a little restructuring. And that's okay.

Of course, it can be difficult to coordinate schedules sometimes, and it may be hard to see people as much as you want. Still, there are plenty of ways to connect with people in between get-togethers. Personally, I found a lot of comfort on online breakup forums such as reddit.com/r/breakups. The first time I went there I discovered there were countless people from all around the world who were going through the same thing I was, and best of all, they had all banded together online to help each other through it. I was able to read other people's stories, talk to them about what they were going through, and get a few things off my chest as well. Best of all, these were people I could talk to 24/7. Late at night or early in the morning, I could log on and brush off the loneliness for a bit. And the same thing is true for you. No matter the time, there are plenty of people to talk to and learn from on a variety of different forums. Sure, you don't know them, and they don't know you, but they know exactly what you're dealing with, and that can make you feel even more connected.

Set Weekly Goals

It's hard to move ahead when you keep looking in the past. That's why we need to make sure you stay focused on your future and keep your sights set on what's ahead of you. One of the best ways to do that is to start setting some simple goals. We're not talking about a 5-year plan here. For right now, all you have to worry about is the week directly ahead of you. Just one week. When Monday or Tuesday rolls around, set a few goals. Write them down, preferably. Whatever goals you choose, though, make sure they are big enough to matter but small enough to accomplish in six or seven days. Learn the entire French language in a week? That's a little too difficult. Eat an entire plate of French toast? That's a little too easy. Deliciously easy. Instead, set a goal to read a book, create something, hit the gym a certain number of times, tackle some big chores, or plan to volunteer two or three nights a week. By focusing on your goals, you'll focus on your breakup less. You'll also have something to look forward to throughout the week. And let's not forget the sweet, sweet sense of satisfaction you'll feel when you accomplish something you've set your mind to.

As the weeks go by, and you see what you can accomplish, you'll start to gain more and more confidence in yourself. If you can accomplish a lot of small things, you'll eventually accomplish big things. Week after week, set your goals, pick a deadline, and get to work. Soon, you'll realize that you can truly move mountains if you want to. All you have to do is move one pebble at a time.

Turn on Some Music

Music can be medicine. Besides getting your toe tapping, we now know that music can heal brain damage, reduce pain, lower anxiety, help with addictions, and balance your brain chemistry.[345] It really is a form of medicine, and best of all, it's inexpensive, prescription-free, and the only needles involved are used for scratching records. That's a plus in my book. One of the reasons music is so powerful is that it stimulates the release of dopamine in your brain.[6] Dopamine is the neurotransmitter best known for creating feelings of pleasure and reward, and that's something you could use right now. By listening to music, you'll counteract some of those negative chemicals circling your brain and lessen those addictive cravings. It won't take all of the pain away, but for me, it made everything a little bit more bearable.

So what should you listen to? First off, skip the radio. Somehow, radio DJs know exactly what songs you absolutely don't want to hear right now, and they'll band together and play those songs non-stop on every channel. Instead, make your own personal playlist, fill it with songs you love, and then listen to them until your earbuds break. If you're not sure what to listen to right this second, start with songs you used to like long before you met your ex – preferably, songs that remind you of some good times gone by.

Think Twice About Getting Back Together

If you've ever watched a romantic comedy before, it might seem like it's your job to win your ex back right now. You might feel an overwhelming urge to keep fighting for her – like this is your chance to prove yourself. All you have to do is to show her how much you care, maybe serenade her in public, or shout your love from the rooftops like they do in the movies. Then she'll realize how you feel, you'll get back together, and your relationship will be stronger than ever. Right? I'm sorry, friend, but no. Those movies should be classified as Fantasy and placed next to The Lord of the Rings.

The truth is, the vast majority of relationships that break in real life can never be put back together, no matter how hard you try.

Researchers from Kansas State University studied couples who had broken up and gotten back together, but the results weren't pretty. Even though these couples had gotten back together, rekindled their romance, and enjoyed some momentary happiness, the breakup they had gone through previously had actually damaged their relationship on a deep level. They didn't usually realize it at first, but huge factors in any relationship, such as trust and emotional intimacy, had been shattered, and the researchers found that people in these relationships had:

- Overall less satisfaction with their partner
- Worse communication
- Lower personal self-esteem
- Anxiety about the future of the relationship
- Worse decision-making skills concerning the

relationship

These are not the kinds of things you want in your life, but many people still get back together after a breakup thinking that it will fix everything. Unfortunately, the researchers also discovered that, even if these reconciled couples went on to get married later on, they had more conflicts, were less satisfied in their marriage, and were more likely to enter a trial separation within three years than regular couples.[7] Even if they had the best of intentions, like you might have right now, sometimes things just don't work out.

Knowing all of this, if you did happen to get back together with your ex, would it be worth it in the end? After the initial rush, you might realize that you can't fully trust each other. You might both be too hurt and fearful to truly commit and invest in the relationship. The arguments you had before might get even worse and the emotional repercussions even more severe. Every little problem might make you wonder if another breakup is right around the corner. And that's no way to grow as a couple and find happiness together. There's a good chance that this "new" relationship wouldn't be anything like the old one you remember, and with all the above factors weighing on you, it might only lead to a messier separation.

So, does anyone get back together and go on to be even happier than before? Yes, of course, but the research tells us it's a long shot. It's a hail-mary pass to a receiver with a broken ankle, and the worst thing you can do right now is waste your time hoping, wishing, and waiting for her to change her mind. I understand that your brain wants you two back together, that it's difficult being single again, and that your ego would choose reconciliation over rejection any day of the week but getting back together won't solve all of your problems – there's a good chance it'll only create new ones. Instead, try to let her go. Stop waiting and wishing. This isn't a test that you have to win. You don't have to prove anything. By letting her go, you're simply doing what's best for yourself, and that means accepting that this particular relationship is behind you. I know this can be tough to hear. In fact, this is one of the hardest things you will do, but this is what acceptance is all about. This is how you truly move on.

Get Some Exercise

Hitting the gym might be the most common piece of advice you'll receive during your breakup, so I apologize if I just got cliché all over your place. Still, when you're going through a breakup, working out just works. We now have a ton of evidence that exercise can actually treat mild to moderate depression because it floods your body with good-time neurotransmitters. In fact, exercising is so effective at treating depression that it's comparable to going to therapy sessions or taking antidepressant medication.[8] That's big news, and exercise has also been proven to help melt away stress, normalize sleep patterns, and help control addictions.[9] In short, exercise is recovery gold.

After my breakup, I started jogging every night, and I will tell you that it did wonders for me. Here's the thing you have to remember though – in the state you're in right now, you're never going to "feel up to it." You'll never be so bursting with energy that you'll want to go running across the country Forrest Gump-style. You simply have to keep reminding yourself that, when you get back from your run, you are going to feel so, so, so much better.

Whatever you do, don't sit around and wait for motivation to strike you. Do not wait for a burst of energy that will never come. There is no "perfect" time. Unless you are injured or sick, you just have to get your shoes on and get out there. Take all those crappy emotions with you and shake them off with each step. Once you hit the pavement, you'll realize that you've gotten past the hardest part already.

So how much exercise is enough? Most of the studies prescribed 30 minutes of aerobic exercise, 3 to 5 days a week. That's a good goal to have, but you don't have to start there. Back then, I couldn't run 30 minutes straight unless I was getting chased by a swarm of bees, so don't sweat it if you get sweaty after two minutes. Try to challenge yourself a little, but don't go overboard. Even if you can only take a few steps today, you're still moving forward. And you'll only improve as time goes by.

Reach Out If You Need Help

The simple act of smiling has been proven to make people feel better.[10] That's why I wrote this book to be upbeat and potentially humorous. If one of these quips in here can make you feel a tiny, tiny bit better, than it's worth it to me to keep on telling them. Still, underneath it all, I truly understand how serious a breakup can be, and I wanted to talk to you seriously about getting help if you find yourself becoming overwhelmed by these emotions.

As I explained in the first chapter, right now your brain chemistry is working against you. It's making you feel terrible and miserable, but it won't last forever. Still, some people get hit by these chemicals harder than other people do. If you find yourself completely overwhelmed by these emotions and you're unsure that things will ever get better, I want you to know that this is not your fault and it's nothing to be ashamed of. There are two reasons why this could be happening – you may be biologically more susceptible to these chemicals because of your genetics, or events in your childhood may have intertwined rejection with other negative emotions like shame or guilt or even feelings of being in danger. Whether it's genetics or upbringing, it's important to remember that neither of these things are your fault. Both were decided far beyond your control, and therefore you shouldn't hold them against yourself or feel too embarrassed to find help for them. If you ever feel like things are becoming too much to bear, or you don't see any light in the distance, I would urge you to seek out a therapist or psychiatrist to discuss these issues. They will be able to address your specific situation and personal needs, and as you already know, simply talking to another person is very helpful during a breakup.

I know it can be hard to ask for help sometimes, but as Marcus Aurelius, the Roman Emperor and definition of manliness, once wrote, "Don't be ashamed to need help. Like a soldier storming a wall, you have a mission to accomplish. And if you have been wounded and you need a comrade to pull you up? So what?"

Exactly, so what?

We all stumble from time to time, and we can either fall to the ground alone, or we can lean on someone for a moment, regain our balance, and keep moving forward.

CHAPTER 3
- Things to Think About -

If you pressed your face up against this book right now, everything would be blurry, nothing would make sense, and eventually, you'd get a headache. The same is true with your breakup. At this point, you're way too close to it, and it's only making things more and more confusing. What you need right now is some perspective, and that's what this chapter is all about. It's filled with things that I wish I knew when I was in the thick of it – things that took me months and even years to realize on my own. Instead of making you wait the old-fashioned way, however, this chapter is a well-needed shortcut that will help you right from the get-go.

What Would Justin Timberlake Do?

People take breakups very personally. It feels like a rejection of everything we are, everything we stand for, and it's very easy to start doubting our own self-worth. But when it comes down to it, this breakup is not a reflection of your inner value. You were not judged by a panel of experts and found lacking. You were not tested alongside the rest of humanity and found inferior. Your ex decided one day that you and her weren't right for each other. And that's it. That's the bottom line. That's the only thing this breakup really means. Her decision to breakup with you was based strictly on your compatibility with her, not on your internal value or what you are capable of. You simply weren't the right match for her, and that's okay. That's a chance we all have to take to find the right person. And everyone goes through it. Of course, you might be thinking, "If only I was richer, or better looking, or more successful, then this wouldn't have happened, right?"

Wrong. You could be rich and famous, but if you're not the right one for her, then there's nothing you can do. If you don't believe me, take Justin Timberlake for example. Yes, *the* Justin Timberlake. A long, long time ago in a bleached-blonde land called the '90s, Justin was topping the charts with his band, N' Sync. He was rich, talented, good looking, charming, funny, and loved around the world. Let's be honest here, the guy was a catch.

Unfortunately for his millions of female fans, JT was already taken by another pop superstar, Britney Spears. They were the quintessential celebrity couple at the time. They bought a house together, walked red carpets hand in hand, performed live in front of huge audiences, and made headliner TV appearances. Basically, everything seemed to be going really, really great for them – right up until the point where they broke up out of nowhere.

To the entertainment world's dismay, after three years together, Justin and Britney suddenly called it quits. Newspapers, magazines and TV shows all picked up the story and rumors began flying that Britney had cheated on Justin with one of her choreographers. During that time, Justin was tight-lipped about the cause of the breakup, but we now know his song "Cry Me a River," a song about an unfaithful lover, was inspired by Britney.[11]

If all the stories surrounding the affair are true though, you have to ask yourself, was Justin not good enough for her? Did he not release enough #1 singles? Did he not have enough money? Should he have won more awards? Was he not good looking enough? Of course, not. What it all comes down to is that they simply weren't right for each other. Justin had a lot of amazing qualities, but Britney wanted something different. Not better by any means. Just different. The same is true in your relationship. You could have had it all, but if your ex wanted something different, there's nothing you could have done. There really is no "better" or "worse" when it comes to attraction. A millionaire CEO might sound like a better catch than a working-class hero, but what if that millionaire has to work 80 hours a week? What if the stress of his company makes him distant, cold and no fun to be with? Some women might be fine with that. Many other women wouldn't be. It's simply a matter of personal preference. At the end of the day, we all bring certain things to the table in our relationships, and some people will value those things and other people won't. You could offer one woman total and complete stability in a relationship, and she'd get bored. You could offer the same thing to another woman, and you would be the man of her dreams. The things we value in a relationship are shaped by an immensely complex interplay between our psychology, biology and past experiences. It's not something that can be rationalized or argued with or even understood most of the time. It's simply a part of who we are.

Every woman you meet will have a different value system. Some women will treasure the qualities you offer them, and some will value different things. That's nothing to blame yourself about. It shouldn't detract from your self-worth. If I prefer women with brown hair, that doesn't mean redheads are any less attractive. That's my own inclination. It has nothing to do with them. Your relationship ended because your ex wanted different things, but that doesn't mean you're worth any less. Remember, Britney wanted different things too, but that didn't stop Justin, and it's not going to stop you either. Once Britney was out of the picture, JT went on to win nine Grammys, sell millions of records, star in movies, become one of the most hilarious hosts on SNL, launch his own clothing line, buy part of the Memphis Grizzlies, open his own golf course, become a notable philanthropist, and marry Jessica Biel.

So, what would Justin Timberlake do after a breakup? Basically, anything and everything he wants to. It didn't stop him, and it won't stop you either.

Every Breakup is a Stepping Stone

As you know now, not everyone is compatible, but unfortunately, it can take years to discover that. People are constantly learning about themselves and their partner, and sometimes their values and feelings change. If you were broken up with, that doesn't mean you are unworthy of love. It simply means that you and your ex weren't right for each other. In the end, she could no longer give you the love that you wanted and deserved, and now, you've been given the chance to find a person who can. Instead of being locked in a one-sided relationship where your ex wasn't fully committed, you two broke up. And even though that hurts like hell, isn't that for the best? I know you may want her back

48

desperately right now, but if she was unable to fully and truly love you, for whatever reason, shouldn't the relationship end? You deserve to spend your time with someone who loves you 100%, values what you have to offer, and doesn't have one foot dangling out the door. After all, the pain of this breakup will eventually fade, but the pain of staying in a loveless relationship will hurt you every day. If your ex was no longer willing to fight for your relationship, if she wanted something different, then it's better to leave her behind.

True, you have to deal with the biological effects of heartache, but there is a bright side to all of this. Fact is, you have never been better equipped to find the right woman than after this breakup. This experience has definitely been painful, but it's given you valuable insight into what to look for in your next relationship. Maybe your ex had a temper. Maybe she never took an interest in the things you liked. Maybe she was unadventurous or unsupportive. In any case, you now have a better understanding of what you really want in a partner and what will make you happy in a relationship. And by breaking up, you now have the chance to find that right person.

But wait, there's more. Not only have you learned what you want in a partner, you've also learned how to BE a better partner. You probably made mistakes during your relationship, but in the chewy nougat center of every mistake is a valuable lesson to be learned. Those little problems and arguments that you had with your ex? You can fix them in the future. Looking back, maybe you need to communicate more. Maybe you need to be more affectionate. Maybe you need to be more spontaneous. When you do find the right person, the person that values you, all the lessons you've learned from this breakup will help make your future relationship even more amazing. And won't that be worth it in the end?

I know breakups are terrible and painful, but let me ask you this: If you could find a woman who truly made you happy, who you enjoyed spending every moment with, who shared your interests and loved you inside and out, how many breakups would you go through to find her – to find that perfect woman for you?

Five?

Ten?

Twenty?

No matter how many it took, wouldn't it all be worth it in the end? Wouldn't she be worth it? When you eventually found this woman, wouldn't you look back, smile, and say it all happened for a reason? Would you even care that you went through all of this right now? No, you would think that this breakup was a blessing. And in many ways, it is. In the end, each breakup is just a stepping stone to the right relationship. You learn what to look for in a partner, and you learn how to be a better partner. The truth is, because of this breakup, you're more prepared to find the right woman than you've ever been before.

There's Never Been a Better Time to Be Single

Of course, I understand that finding the right woman right now might seem like a giant steaming cup of never gonna happen. You're might be feeling awful. Your confidence and trust might still be reeling. Maybe you're not sleeping. Maybe the only woman you want to think about is your ex. I get it, but there's a reason I'm so confident that you can find the right person. Actually, there are several reasons, and even though you're not thinking about dating right now, I wanted to give you a little sneak peek at what you have to look forward to.

Fact is, there are more single women around today than there has ever been in the history of the universe. And that's a long time. There are literally billions of women out there, and just for clarification, a billion is far larger than most people usually realize. To give you some perspective, if you started counting seconds right now, it would take you twelve days to reach a million. Twelve days may seem like a long time, in terms of seconds, but if you wanted to count to a billion, it would take you 31 years. Yes, years. Suffice it to say, a billion is a huge number, and that is just one of the reasons I am so confident that you can find the right person. The numbers speak for themselves. As it turns out, your ex didn't breakup with you, she simply tossed you into an endless ocean of interesting and attractive women.

And if sheer quantity wasn't good enough, it's easier than ever to find a quality relationship too. Today, there are more activities to do. More clubs. More ways to connect with people. It's easier to travel. Easier to communicate. There are more events. More ways to have fun. And more ways to spend your time. If you like rock climbing, there are more climbing gyms than ever. If you're into music, there are more bands, concerts, and more ways to interact with fellow fans.

Since there are more things to do, there are

more ways to meet women who share your particular interests. Let's face it, if you lived in a tiny mountain village in 400BC, finding the right woman would be a tough proposition. You'd probably be forced to marry your second cousin. You'd have nothing to talk about besides your fear of the plague. The only thing you'd have in common would be, like, eating a ton of cabbage every day. And you'd spend the rest of your life just grinning and bearing it. Nowadays, it doesn't matter how hot your second cousin is, you've got plenty of other options. The world is wide open to you. You can go out there and find a woman who truly shares your interests and ideals.

And oh yeah, the internet's got your back as well. As I said earlier, we all have certain qualities, and it's just a matter of finding someone who values the ones you have (and vice versa). Online dating was created for this specific purpose. You can now find someone who shares your interests and life goals without handing a questionnaire to every woman you see on the street. Today, one in three Americans meet their spouses online, and the research suggests that these people have more fulfilling marriages on average than those couples who met in person first.[12]

Online, offline, or waiting in line for a show, there's no right way to meet the right person, but I wanted to give you a glimpse at the limitless opportunities that are awaiting you. True, your relationship with one woman may be over, but that's only one woman out of billions. The odds are ridiculously in your favor that you'll find the right one someday.

CHAPTER 4
- Becoming Unbreakable -

Before you do a spectacular cannonball back into the dating pool, of course, it's a good idea to spend some time focusing on yourself, building your confidence back up, and finding out what you're truly capable of. After all, I don't want you to simply get over this breakup, I want you to skyrocket above it. I want you to take all of these powerful emotions you're feeling right now, turn them away from the darkside, and use them as a powerful motivator to better yourself and your life. I want you to come out of this breakup better than you were before, and someday, be grateful it all went down the way it did.

So what's this chapter all about? In a word – you. It's about finding out who you are now that you're single. It's about rebuilding your confidence and self-esteem, and taking your first steps to a brighter, unbreakable future. Sure, you could kick back, let all those techniques in Chapter Two work their sweet healing magic, but why stop there? Every breakup is a wake-up call. It's a terrible 5:00 AM wake-up call after a night of binge drinking, but it's a wake-up call nonetheless. It's the perfect time to ask yourself what do you really want to do, where do you want to go, and what kind of man do you really want to be. It's an opportunity to focus on yourself and discover your true potential. Will it take work? Hot damn yes. Will it take time? That's for sure. But it's going to take time for your biological addiction to fade anyway. Why not spend that time working, instead of just waiting. Why not give yourself something to focus on besides your ex. Why not make this breakup the best thing that's ever happened to you. If you're willing to work, if you're willing to invest in yourself, then this is the chapter for you.

The Four Foundations of Confidence

Breakups can do a number on your confidence. I'm not sure what that number is, but I'm guessing it's somewhere around -1,000,000 Metric Confidence Units. Unfortunately, that can be a real problem as you move forward. As I'm sure you know, confidence is king. It's one of the most important attributes a guy can possess. Research tells us that it makes us better leaders and better athletes, it can lead to more success at work and higher salaries during our careers, and survey after survey says that it's one of the most attractive attributes a man can possess. This is why I included this chapter. Even if you were to completely get over your ex tomorrow, it wouldn't be much of a recovery if your confidence was still in shambles. So, instead of waiting for it to naturally return some day, we're going to give your confidence a little kickstart.

Now, there are a variety of ways to build up your confidence. There are shelves and shelves of books on the subject and plenty of different techniques you can use. There are affirmations you can say, you can write brag lists, leave yourself compliment notes, focus on your good qualities, but for me, nothing works better than simply getting up and getting to work. That's where the four foundations of confidence come into play. These are the four most efficient areas you can work on to directly boost your confidence...

Wealth	Achievements
Appearance	Social Circle

You don't have to excel in all of these areas to be confident, of course. You may be strong in a few of these areas already. These are simply the best places to invest your time and energy to build a sturdy foundation of confidence that isn't easily swayed by outside opinion or influence.

For example, imagine if you asked a woman out, and for one reason or another, she said no. If you didn't have a solid foundation of confidence to fall back on, that rejection would hit you like a ton of feathers (which is just as bad as a ton of bricks). On the other hand, if you had accomplished many of your goals, had a career you enjoyed, felt good inside and out, and had good friends to rely on, getting rejected might still be disappointing, but it wouldn't take away from anything you've accomplished. All those things you've worked for and achieved would still be with you. By putting time and energy into yourself, you would have learned to value yourself. You would have developed a strong sense of self-worth, and best of all, your confidence would no longer be at the whim of other people's opinions. Instead, it would be entirely dictated by your own opinion. And that's what becoming unbreakable is all about. It's about building confidence that's innate, internal, and doesn't rely on external validation. Instead of taking that rejection personally and blaming your own shortcomings, you would simply dust off your shoulders and get back to being awesome. No harm done.

So how does working on yourself lead to self-worth? If I had to explain it in a metaphor, I'd say it's very similar to restoring a classic car. Week after week you work and work. Nights and weekends, you're out in that garage replacing parts, removing panels, sandblasting rust, tightening and untightening countless bolts. Months and months go by, but eventually things start to take shape. You end up putting your everything into that car, and by the time the paint's shining and the engine's purring, you love that thing. All that time, all that effort, has made it valuable to you – more valuable than any other car could be. You're proud of it, you're protective of it, and you take great care of it because you know first-hand what it took to build it.

When you start investing time and energy into yourself, the same thing happens. You work. You toil. And eventually, things start to take shape. You begin to value yourself because you know exactly how much effort you've put into yourself. As the months go by, you start to admire the person you're becoming. You're proud of everything you've accomplished. And eventually, that inner pride turns into real confidence that has a positive influence on everything you do. In fact, it might just be the best return on investment you'll ever find.

So how do you get started? If your breakup was pretty recent, give it about a month or two. Don't jump into anything too soon. You should be feeling better, your emotions should be more stable, and you should have all those techniques in Chapter Two down to a T before you begin. Once you're feeling decent-ish, start thinking about which foundations you want to focus on. You can pursue one of them at a time, or a few all at once. It really depends on your personal strengths and what you're interested in. Before we go any further, let's discuss each foundation in detail:

Wealth: Mo' money doesn't always mean mo' problems. In fact, doing good work and being paid well for it can generate a lot of confidence. Money itself can raise your quality of life and provide you with security and stability. Having money to fall back on can also reduce a lot of financial stress and worry that would otherwise sap your confidence. Most importantly though, earning money by utilizing your personal talents can be extremely satisfying. Instead of earning a paycheck for simply showing up, every dollar becomes a testament to your ability and dedication. And with that comes a wonderful kind of confidence.

There are a few ways to build on this foundation. You could focus on getting a raise or promotion at your current job, change jobs or careers altogether to something that better fits your abilities, or even start your own side business. Of course, none of these things are easy. This foundation is the most difficult to focus on, and it's definitely not the best one to jump into right after a breakup. In other words, don't up and quit your job on me. Take your time with this one. Think things through, but later down the road, start to ask yourself if you're taking full advantage of your skills. Are you being compensated fairly? Are you grabbing hold of all the opportunities available to you? A recent *Forbes* article found that if you stay at your job for more than two years, instead of moving around and negotiating higher and higher salaries, you'll earn 50% less over the course of your lifetime.[13] A job change might not be right for you, but these are the types of things you should look into and start considering as time goes by.

Achievements: This foundation is all about making you a more interesting, well-rounded person. The achievement you focus on can be almost anything from scaling a mountain, learning a new skill, or overcoming a specific challenge in your life. It all depends on what you're interested in and what your strengths are. To get the most bang for your buck though, your achievement should meet some basic criteria:

1. It should challenge you appropriately.
2. It should better you in some way.
3. It should make you proud of yourself.

To simplify things, if someone asks you what you've been up to lately, you should be able to proudly tell them what you've been working on. You should be able to brag about it a little. Basically, don't spend next weekend putting together a 100,000-piece jigsaw puzzle. Yes, it would be challenging. Yes, you might be weirdly proud of it. But I've never seen someone brag about their jigsaw skills before. At least not successfully.

Instead, learn how to cook, enter a race, travel

somewhere exotic, start volunteering, create something new, learn to dance, take a class or attend a workshop. If you've always been afraid of talking in front of large crowds, getting over that fear would be a great achievement as well. Or maybe you want to quit smoking or break some other bad habit. All of these things would be worth boasting about. Whatever you choose to do, simply keep improving. Keep developing. After all, the more interests you have, the more interesting you are.

Appearance: It's time to discuss the elephant man in the room. Looks do matter. But probably not in the way you think. When it comes down to it, studies have shown that the way we view our own appearance is far more important than what anybody else says or thinks. In fact, feeling good about your own looks is the single, strongest predictor in determining your overall self-esteem.[14] Luckily for us, the two biggest factors in determining your appearance – your style and your shape – are completely under your control. You can change your style. You can change your shape. The way you look is not set in stone. In truth, being handsome isn't something you have to be born with or something you luck into. A poll of women done by *Men's Health Magazine* found that a "sense of style" was the most attractive physical trait a man can possess.[15] Well, guess what? There's no one forcing you to wear denim jumpsuits every day of your life. You can improve your style at any time with a little research and work. And the same is true for the shape of your body.

If you decide this foundation is for you, you can tackle both style and shape at the same time. Working on your style would include things like getting new clothes, changing up your haircut, possibly getting a new pair of glasses if you wear them, and even improving your body language. I would also include things like seeing a dermatologist, if you want to improve your skin, keeping your beard and body hair trimmed, making sure your breath is up to snuff and sniff, and possibly, test driving a few designer colognes. Of course, they say the clothes make the man, so that should be your main focus. The internet is crawling with fashion guides, so you should be in good hands, but it can take some work. A lot of fashion you will find in magazines and blogs is a little too avant-garde for most people's taste. Personally, you'd never catch me wearing white capri pants with sockless loafers, a velvet blazer and an orange infinity scarf. Have I seen it in a fashion mag? Yes. Would I want to wear it to the supermarket? Not exactly. Thankfully, clothing stores themselves tend to be a little less experimental. If you're looking for a new outfit, a good idea is to find a few stores you like, go to their websites, and see which outfits they put on their models. After all, they've hired real wardrobe stylists to put these outfits together. Once you've spent some time window shopping, you should be able to tell what kind of pants look best with which kind of shirt, and what kind of shoes and belt match as well. From there, you can start putting together an entire wardrobe, and even start dabbling in white capri pants, if you really want to.

Style can be tricky, I admit, but your shape is another story altogether. Changing your body isn't as fast as changing a pair of jeans. It takes time. It takes effort. But it is one of the most satisfying goals you can focus on, and it has benefits like you wouldn't believe. If you decide to start exercising to slim down or tone up, you're going to be enjoying a laundry-list of perks, including:

- A lower risk of heart disease (the leading cause of death in the US)
- A lower risk for certain cancers (the second leading cause of death in the US)
- A lower risk of having a stroke (the fourth leading cause of death in the US)
- Less chance of depression
- More energy throughout the day
- Better sleep throughout the night
- Improved brain function
- An increased libido and less chance of erectile dysfunction[16]

A list like that is hard to argue with, and on top of all that, working consistently to eat right and exercise also gives you a great feeling of forward momentum starting the very first week. So where to begin? There are more workout programs and routines out there than there are muscles in your body, so it can be tough deciding which one to choose. When you start out, don't go throwing your money at the first program that promises amazing results. There is a ton of low-cost to no-cost information out there if you're just starting out. Bodybuilding.com is loaded with info for beginners. Reddit.com/r/fitness has a great FAQ. I would also look into intermittent fasting for weight loss, Couch-to-5k if you want to work on cardio, or check out Push-Pull-Lift programs or Starting Strength if you're looking to bulk up. These programs will cover the basics. Of course, the most important thing to remember is that your diet plays the absolute biggest role in changing your shape. As they say, bodies aren't built in the gym, they are built in the kitchen. Before you begin an exercise program please spend the time, do some research, and make sure you understand how much you need to eat to get the results you're looking for.

Whatever program you choose, whether it's at home or in a gym, make sure you can stick with it for at least three months. Be honest with yourself. If the program is too intense, too complicated, costs too much money, requires too much driving, or forces you to lose sleep, one day you're going to give it up. Choose a program that you know you can stick with, the one with the least obstacles, and then devote yourself to it. If you want to build a better body, you have to be in it for the long haul. After three months, you should see definite improvement, but it can take upwards of six months to a year to get the results you really want, depending on where you started from and where you want to go. Still, three to six months is a small price to pay to feel confident, strong, and healthy, not to mention feeling more attractive and enjoying all those benefits I mentioned above.

No matter what fitness goals you have or what you decide to wear, remember, it all comes down to how you view yourself. Wear what you think looks good. Build the body you think is attractive. Don't worry about meeting other people's expectations, simply strive to meet your own. In the end, your own opinion about yourself is the only opinion that truly matters.

Social Circle: As social creatures, we thrive when we have a strong social circle we can rely on. People with a large network of friends tend to live longer, have higher self-esteem, better immune systems, and lower levels of cortisol.[17] Friends also provide you with a sense of security, support you when times get rough, and give you opportunities to grow and better yourself. All of which can lead to greater and greater confidence, which is why I've included here.

If you want to focus on this foundation, and round out your social circle, there are two ways to go about it: you can spend time strengthening old relationships or you can focus on building brand new ones. In either case, you simply have to spend time with people. You can start by hanging out with old friends more, you can throw an invite out to a few acquaintances and see what happens, or you can go out there and make some friends from scratch.

If you do decide to make new friends, research has found that the two most important factors in forming a friendship are 1) common interests and 2) chances for repeated, no-pressure contact. That's why it was so easy to make friends in elementary school. You both saw each other every day, and you were both really into chicken nuggets. Great friendships were bound to happen at that point. Now that you're older and nuggets aren't the hot topic they used to be, you can either make friends at work, where you live, or you can start doing activities that will allow you to see the same people over and over again. This means things like volunteering where there are a number of people, joining a class where there is time for social interaction, or joining an intramural team. This will give you the repetition you need in a no-pressure environment with people who share your interests.

Whichever method you choose, the key to having good friends, really, is to be a good friend yourself. Stick up for them when other people won't. Be there for them when times get rough. Encourage them when they need it. By loyal. Be trustworthy. Basically, be the kind of friend you would like to have, and the rest will fall into place eventually. Maybe not with the first person you meet, but definitely in due time.

* * *

Those are the four foundations for you. Hopefully, you've got a good understanding of them, but now you might be asking yourself, "When am I going to have time to do all this stuff?" That's a good question, and we've got strategies to make it work.

The best way to fit these foundations into your life is to tackle a few of them at the same time, during the same activity. For example, you could work out alone to enhance your appearance. Or better yet, you could take classes at an MMA gym to get fit, achieve something to be proud of, and grow your social circle all at the same time. That's three foundations for the time investment of one. Another example: you could go to meetup.com, join a hiking group and end up getting in shape, scaling mountains, and making some new friends while you're at it. Have you always wanted to learn how to cook? You could read a book, of course, or you could double-up on foundations and ask a family member or a friend to teach you in person. Tell them you'll pick up the groceries, if they'll spend the time to walk you through a recipe. Very few people will say no to that offer, and you'll probably learn more from hands-on instruction, you'll have more fun, and you'll also strengthen your social circle at the same time. Whichever foundations you want to focus on, try your best to hit a few of them at once.

If you're racking your brain, and a foundation combo package is completely out of the question, another trick is to simply start setting goals. Reaching a personal goal will allow you build on your achievement foundation without any extra work. Say you want to exercise alone. Right from the get-go, give yourself a small goal to aim for. Maybe you want to reach a certain weight, add another plate to your deadlift, or improve your run time or distance. Once you hit your goal, not only will you have worked to better your appearance, but you will have achieved something as well. That's two foundations right there, and it will feel far more rewarding than exercising without a goal in sight. From there, give yourself another goal, go after it, and let your confidence skyrocket.

Of course, no matter how many foundations you manage to hit at once, you still need some time to do them. A lesson you should focus on during this period, if you haven't mastered it already, is to start filling your free time with active leisure instead of losing hours and hours to passive leisure. Passive leisure includes things like watching TV or movies, playing video games, endlessly scrolling on TikTok, or anything else that's easy, requires little engagement or concentration and doesn't better us in any way. Strangely enough, research has shown that these passive activities, like watching TV, are only enjoyable for around 30 minutes.

After that time, people report decreased enjoyment and satisfaction, but because these activities are so unchallenging, readily available, and we're already doing them, we simply keep at it – even when we've stopped enjoying them all together. We get sucked in, and suddenly all of our free time disappears. Active leisure, on the other hand, involves exercising, learning, creating and exploring – all things that could build on your foundations. These activities engage us, leave us feeling fulfilled, improve our skills, and most impressively, are typically <u>three times</u> more enjoyable than simply sitting around and watching TV.[18]

Now I understand how appealing it is to come home from work or school and spend hours lazing around the house. I did it so much I think my spirit animal might be a three-toed sloth with an Ambien addiction, but looking back now, I realize I overdid it. Fact is, there are some shows, movies and video games that are well worth watching and playing. They expand our minds, give us new perspectives, and truly grip us, but those kinds of experiences are few and far between. Honestly, the vast majority of passive entertainment we get sucked into isn't that great to begin with and is merely an easy way to waste time. How many bad movies have you watched in your life? How many barely-entertaining video games have you played? You probably can't remember, and that's exactly the point. We end up losing months and years of our lives to mediocre, forgettable entertainment, and in the end, we have nothing to show for it. If I asked you to write your bucket list right now, would it include things like, "watch every episode of an average sitcom" or "spend months questing for the glowing sword in some generic fantasy game?" Of course not, and yet, that's what many of us end up doing. The average American spends 34 hours a week watching TV.[19] And that's before we add in video games, movies, and unproductive web browsing. Imagine all the amazing things you could accomplish with that much time. Unfortunately, passive leisure is so easy that we tend to do it far more often. And since we do it more often, it eventually becomes a habit, and from there, we are naturally drawn to repeat it time and time again, even if we'd rather be doing something else. If this cycle of passive leisure is standing between you and getting what you want out of life, this is the perfect time to do away with it once and for all. Lucky enough, your breakup is actually going to do you a huge favor in this case.

Approximately 45% of our everyday behaviors are habitual.[20] Your brain creates these behavior patterns so that you don't have to struggle to brush your teeth every morning. You don't have to think to yourself – up then down, up then down. You just do it. It becomes automatic. And while habits are good for remembering how to tie your shoes and put on pants, other habits have us flipping through channels for hours, or browsing the same apps over and over again. These habits of passive leisure have been repeated so often that they've become ingrained in us and are usually hard to break.

Usually, but not always.

Turns out, the best time to change a habit or create a new one is directly after a large life event.[21] These events include moving, having a baby, getting a new job, and oh yes, going through a breakup. These life events are like a habit reset switch. For example, if you drank coffee in the office break room every morning at 8:00am, but you ended up getting an entirely new job that doesn't start until 9:00, then your old habit would have to be broken. There's no way around it, and your brain understands this. Your brain is programmed to become more flexible when it realizes big things have changed, and it will allow you to alter or form new habits far easier than normal. This holds true during breakups as well. Any foundation you want to pursue, any habits you want to change, anything you want to achieve, your brain's giving you the go ahead to get it done right now. When I said this breakup could be one of the best things that's ever happened to you, I wasn't drunk on hyperbole. I meant it. You have the motivation, you know what to focus on, and you now have the chance to rewire all of your bad habits. Opportunity isn't just knocking right now, it's kicking your door in. It's telling you to go forth, to accomplish great things, and to get the most out of life.

And really, is there any goal greater than that?

If you've ever followed boxing, there's a saying you may have heard – leave it all in the ring. It's a simple reminder that every fighter only gets so many rounds. During that time, they have to give it everything they've got, never lose heart, and keep fighting, so that when that final bell rings, they can look back with no regrets. Breakups aside, if I could give you one piece of life advice, it would be the same six words – leave it all in the ring. On your 99th birthday, I want you to look down at that blinding, candle-covered birthday cake in front of you and know that you took those years for all they were worth. You pushed yourself, challenged yourself. You refused to take the easy path. Instead, you did wondrous things, loved amazing people, saw beautiful sights, and even though it was far more difficult than watching TV, you used your time and talents to better yourself and the lives of those around you. To me, that's a life well spent and something you can truly be proud of.

So does that mean you should chuck your TV out of the nearest window right this second? Probably! Wait, wait, I meant no. Passive leisure still has its place, of course. After all, you can't spend every waking moment working out or learning new things. You don't have to push yourself 110% all day, every day. We all need some downtime from time to time, but the key is to find a balance. Instead of TV or video games being your go-to activity, your natural fallback, treat those things like a reward. Veg out *after* hitting the gym. Laze around *after* working on your personal project. Earn those moments of leisure, instead of overindulging on them. If you're like the average American and spend around 40 hours a week on passive leisure, simply cut that in half and spend 20 of those hours being productive. You'll still catch the best shows, you'll still play the best games, and you'll still have time to recharge and refresh. But by adding in active leisure, you'll feel more fulfilled at the end of the day, you'll have more fun, and over time, you'll get real things done – things you can look back on for years to come.

Avoid the Rebound Relationship

There's another way to save plenty of time, and

that's simply by being single. All those hours you spent with your ex, hanging out with her, doing things for her, or taking her out can now be spent on yourself. And those hours add up quick. By being single, and staying single, you're probably going to have a fair amount of time on your hands. I will be honest with you though. Research has shown that finding a new partner is actually the single best way to get over a breakup.[22] Now, that may sound like a reason to go out right now and date as many women as possible, all the while saying, "Science made me do it!"

But hold on.

Finding a new partner should definitely be one of your end-goals but getting into a relationship too soon can backfire big time. It's tempting to find someone new, remove those feelings of rejection, and enjoy a nice ego boost while you're at it, but you might end up settling for whoever's available, not who you really want to be with. You might lead someone on, use them to inflate your ego, and then end up having to toss them aside later on. My advice – don't be that guy. It's selfish, it wastes your time, and it'll only end up hurting the other person. If you're fresh out of breakup, it's a good idea to swear off new relationships for at least a few months. You're strong enough to go it alone for a time, and in this short period, you'll also learn three very valuable lessons:

1. You'll learn how to be alone. During this period, you'll realize that being alone isn't as bad as some people make it out to be. You can do whatever you want, whenever you want, and you don't have to be held back by your partner's expectations. Being single can be scary, but it's also extremely liberating. If you want to go for a hike, see a movie, hit the gym, cook something special, or take a weekend trip, you can just go for it. You don't have to align schedules or make sure your girlfriend is up for it. You make the rules now.

Most importantly, by learning how to be alone, you'll never be afraid to leave a bad relationship in the future. So many people get stuck in the wrong relationship simply because they are afraid to be single, but that's no way to live. Fear shouldn't be the driving emotion in any relationship. Give it a few months, and you'll start to understand that it's okay to be alone, that it's better to be single than to be with the wrong person, and having that mindset will make every one of your relationships richer.

2. You'll learn how to focus on yourself. To build your confidence back up, it's going to take time and it's going to take work. If you jump into another relationship too soon, you're not going to have the time to truly invest in yourself and discover what you're capable of. This breakup is the perfect opportunity to put yourself first, to make your dreams a priority, and to find out what you really want out of life – without another person swaying your opinion. In a long relationship, people often get cornered by their partner's expectations. They are afraid to change or grow or try new things because they don't want to rock the boat. At the same time, long relationships can leave people unmotivated and complacent. They get comfortable with things simply being "good," instead of making them great. They have no huge problems, challenges, or hurdles to face, so they have no reason to push themselves.

You, my friend, are lucky in this respect. You now have a challenge to overcome. You have a hurdle in your path, but you have the motivation you need to overcome it. By focusing on your future now, rebuilding your confidence, and getting a glimmer of your true potential, you can avoid all those pitfalls of complacency in the future. You can learn to stay driven and motivated, even when you're in a relationship, and that will help you throughout your life.

3. You'll find out who you really are. In long relationships, people's personalities can start to intertwine. Their tastes, dreams, desires, and even their mannerisms can blend together. Now that you're single, you can make sure you're being true to yourself. Maybe you only liked sushi because your ex did. Maybe you were only into volleyball because she was. Maybe you've always wanted to do something or go somewhere, but she was never up for it. Even the jokes you tell or the way you talk might be influenced by your ex, but that will eventually fade. Over time, you'll realize what you, and only you, really enjoy doing and what you really want out of life.

***

So how long should you lone wolf it for? I wish I could give you a solid date, but it really depends on how severe your breakup was and how well you recover. If you're strictly following no contact, it takes about two months to break a physical addiction to an ex. After that, you should add an extra month or two to focus entirely on yourself. That may seem like a long time, but trust me, it goes by in a flash, especially if you're busy working on your foundations.

As the months pass by, you may occasionally feel disheartened though, and I want to address that now. As guys, we're often judged by our ability to attract and seduce women. We feel pressured to either be in a relationship or be dating so many women that we don't have time to commit to one. If you're single and not ready to mingle, it can start to weigh on your self-esteem after a few months. You might start to wonder, "I'm doing all these great things, but I'm still single. Obviously, it's not working. Maybe I should just give up." If these backward thoughts ever come up, I want you to remember a few things.

To start, no truly great man in history has ever been measured by whether or not he had a girlfriend. Ask yourself, how many girlfriends did George Washington have? How many women did Alexander the Great sleep with? Did Shakespeare have groupies? No one cares about these things because they're not important. You'll never open a history book and see the American Presidents listed by how many women they hooked up with in college. Fact is, *what* you do in your life is far more important than *who* you do in your life. If you're single, that doesn't mean you're worth any less. If you're not out there dating woman after woman right now, that doesn't mean you're not good enough. During these few months of bachelordom, don't worry about being single. Right now, it's all about you. The women will come later.

Become the Person You Really Want to Be

I may be plagiarizing about 90% of children's books ever created when I say this, but you can be anything you want to be. And I'm not talking about becoming an astronaut or the next President. I'm talking about becoming the kind of man you've always wanted to be, infused with all the characteristics you admire.

Right now, you're single, and that means you're starting off with a slate so clean you could eat off it. No one's holding you back. There are no strings attached. You can grow in any direction you choose without getting a raised eyebrow from a wife or girlfriend. This can be as simple as getting a new haircut, dressing a different way, learning new skills, or taking on new interests. But it can also mean changing your entire outlook, attitude or behavior.

Many people in relationships tend to conform to their partner's expectations. They fall into routines for the sake of the relationship and put a TBD on who they really want to be. If you were more reserved and shy when you first met your partner, you'd be less inclined to suddenly become a huge extrovert later in the relationship – even if that was something you wanted to be. You'd be worried about disapproval, embarrassment, or introducing tension into the relationship, and so you'd probably stick with what worked and put your personal growth on hold.

It doesn't have to be that way anymore. The only expectations you have to meet now are your own. If there are qualities, attributes or traits you've always admired, you can acquire them too. Maybe you can't become the next President, but you can become adventurous, or outgoing, or sophisticated, or noble, or courageous. You can change almost any internal quality you desire through the simple act of repetition repetition repetition. That may seem farfetched, but this idea has stood the test of time for over 2,000 years. Back during the original toga parties, Aristotle preached this exact message. As he said:

Men acquire a particular quality by constantly acting a particular way. You become just by performing just actions, temperate by performing temperate actions, brave by performing brave actions.

He later summarized this idea in a single sentence, "We are what we repeatedly do." If you want to be a more outgoing person, all you have to do is perform outgoing actions – get out there, do things, be friendly, and strike up conversations. If you want to feel more confident, start acting confidently – stand tall, speak well, look people in the eye, and smile like you get paid by the tooth. It's very simple, but it works. And we even have proof.

Researchers from Columbia and Harvard found that people who posed their bodies in confident, high-power positions for two minutes had elevated levels of testosterone, lower levels of stress hormones, tolerated risk better, and benefited from feelings of power.[23] By merely pretending to be confident, their brain chemistry, their outlook, and their behavior all changed to make them feel more confident. And that's just with a few, two-minute poses. Imagine what would happen if you spent an entire day, or week, or month acting confidently, especially with some solid foundations backing you up.

And you can use this trick for any personal quality you would like to improve, whether it's bravery, patience, dependability, kindness, honesty, or sophistication. You name it. If there's a specific attribute you would like to have, simply act like you already have it, and eventually you will.

Of course, picking and choosing attributes, waiting for an opportunity to use them, and constantly repeating them can get a little complicated. If there's one aspect you really feel needs work, focus on it entirely. Every day, try to do to one action that will improve that quality and eventually you'll own it. For everyone else, I believe Aristotle's message touches on one fundamental lesson that I hope will stick with you:

> *No matter what you do, always act in a way that you, yourself, would admire.*

If you always act in a way that you admire, then you will eventually become someone you admire. You will become the hero of your own story. You will become someone you can look up to. And this will allow you to love and respect yourself, which will lead to self-confidence, self-esteem, and most importantly, happiness. Sure, this can be difficult at times. It means having to take the high road more often than not, but here's the thing with high roads – they may be a lot harder to climb, but in the end, the views are far more spectacular.

As the weeks and months pass by, remember to stand tall, act admirably, invest in yourself, keep growing, keep learning, do what you love, and strive to reach your potential. After all, things are always changing. Friends move away, relationships may come and go, jobs begin and end, but you will always, always have yourself. Whatever you do, make sure he's the kind of person you'd want to hang out with for the rest of your life.

Stay Driven

Someday you're going to find yourself smack dab in the middle of an amazing new relationship. It's going to better than you ever dreamed, you're going to be happy from head to toe, and you're going to want to spend every waking moment together. When that day comes, first off: congrats, you sly dog you. Secondly, despite how tempting it may be at the time, do not give up on your goals. Whatever foundations you're working on, stick with them. Whatever you've set out to achieve, keep at it. By staying driven and staying ambitious, not only will you better yourself, but you'll better your relationship as well.

A classic mistake many guys make is to put their aspirations aside when they get into a relationship. For them, finding the right woman was their main motivation in life. It was what drove them to reach higher, to push further, to get a better job, a nicer body, or a bigger house – not for their own benefit – but merely to attract a woman. It's the reason some guys pick up their first guitar, or buy a flashy sports car, or study hard in school. It's a good incentive for a time, but here's the rub: If finding a girl is your primary motivation, what happens after you find her?

After getting into a relationship, many guys have no idea what to do next. They enjoyed the thrill of finding someone, of course, but as time passes by, their motivation wanes. With a relationship established, they feel like their main mission has been accomplished. They have nothing pushing them anymore, no grand goals to set their sights on, and nothing to inspire them. They end up feeling aimless, unsure what to do next, and eventually, they take the path of least resistance – they become lazy and complacent. Unfortunately, complacency is like spray-on romance-remover, and many of these guys end up sabotaging the very relationship they tried so hard to find.

This isn't the case for everyone, of course, but I believe it's a very common problem for both men and women. Of all the breakup stories I've read (tons), and all the people I've talked to, complacency was the #1 issue I heard, and many times it was the biggest factor in causing a long-term relationship to end. The majority of these stories read exactly the same way. In the beginning, the guy/girl was exciting, adventurous, and charming, which is what made them so attractive to begin with, but as the years passed by, they lost their passion for life, became listless, let themselves go, and settled for a life of monotony. The other partner realized all of this and then jumped ship.

I don't want this to happen to you. And not because it could hurt any future relationship either. Honestly, if a woman wants to leave you because you're in a rut, then it's for the best. For me, personally, I want you to avoid the rut altogether. I don't want you to fall into this trap and settle for a mere existence. I want you to keep striving and pushing yourself even after you've long settled down. Fact is, finding the right woman is a very important goal to have, but it should only be one of the many great things you want to accomplish. It should never be your primary motivation. That's not fair to you or to the woman you end up being with.

So what should you strive for exactly? According to famed psychologist Abraham Maslow, we all have an innate, human desire to be all that we can be and to reach the pinnacle of our potential. As he put it, "What a man *can* be, he *must* be." Whatever you're good at, whatever truly fulfills you, you should make time for and become the best you can be at it. Of course, you don't have to become the world's fastest runner or the greatest painter in history. In truth, this has nothing to do with other people. As Ernest Hemingway said, "There is nothing noble in being superior to your fellow man; true nobility is being superior to your former self." This is about testing and harnessing your own abilities and seeing what you're capable of. And it can include almost anything. You can focus on your athletic ability or your creative talents. You can become the ideal parent, if you have children, or excel at your job if it's something you enjoy. Whatever you're naturally drawn to, it is from this self-actualization that Maslow believed we will find true fulfillment.[24]

Love does have a place in all of this, of course. Maslow believed that love was a fundamental desire, but it was not the end-all of human ambition. In his theory, the Hierarchy of Human Needs, our basic physiological needs like food and water were at the very bottom, followed by security, then love, self-esteem, and at the very top, self-actualizing. Love does play a role, obviously. It gives us strength and courage. It supports us and allows us reach further – to realize our potential. But it's not the ultimate finish line.

When you do find the right woman, treasure each other's company, spend plenty of time relaxing, but remember to keep moving forward together. Don't ditch your dreams. Instead, help each other to fulfill them, lift each other up to great new heights, inspire each other to grow, support each other's passions, and love each other powerfully. In the end, you both will benefit. By supporting each other, you'll grow closer. By being passionate about your goals, you'll bring passion into your relationship. By having a real thirst for life, you'll both share more memories, have more fun, and keep your relationship fresh and exciting. Best of all, you'll still accomplish the things you want to do in life. Only this time, you'll have someone cheering you on the entire way. It's the best of both worlds, and in a relationship like that, complacency doesn't stand a chance.

CHAPTER 5
- The Dear Jane Letter -

With everything you know now, you should have an honorary black belt in getting over breakups, but there's one more step to go. Consider it the official closing ceremonies of your old relationship.

When you feel like you're almost over this breakup, when you're feeling good, and maybe just starting to date again, set aside some time to write a Dear Jane Letter. This is an expressive writing exercise that's often recommended in therapy sessions. Exercises like this have been shown to better your health, improve working memory, increase sports performance, and much more.[25] If you become a better baseball player after this, hey bonus, but the main goal of this letter is to state once and for all that you're done with this breakup. That you're done thinking about it or being manipulated by it. That, after this moment, you've officially moved on to bigger and better things.

When you're ready to write your letter, make sure you have some free time and that you're away from any distractions. Take out a pen and a piece of paper. Address the letter to your ex, and then write everything you've always wanted to say to her. Tell her how you really feel. Tell her about all the great things you've been doing. Tell her you miss her or tell her you can't stand her. Write about the good times you two shared or how much the ending hurt. Tell her how excited you are for the future. Tell her everything and anything, but most importantly, at the very end, tell her goodbye. Even if you still see her from time to time, say goodbye to the girl you once knew and the relationship you were in. This might sting a little. To be honest, I never liked goodbyes either. But this letter is your declaration that you have moved on – that you're over her. And the best way to do that is by saying goodbye.

After you've gotten out everything you want to say, take a moment to reread your letter once again. Don't fight any emotions that spring up. Don't try to suppress anything. This is your time to let it all go and explore anything that comes to the surface.

Then, when you're ready, take your letter, tear it up into little pieces, and toss those scraps into the trash. Do not send it to her. This letter is not meant for her. It's meant for you. And as the last pieces of paper slip out of your fingers, tell yourself that this is it, this breakup is over and done with. Everything's been said. Everything's been felt. You are completely free now.

* * *

Expressive writing like this has been shown to cause some emotional distress at the time, but those feelings go away quickly. Still, you should be ready for them. If you're doing so well in life that you don't want to spend a second looking back, that's fine too. If you think this letter will only slow you down, feel free to skip it. For me, personally, writing a letter like this felt like a true ending to my breakup. Even though I was already feeling great, dating again, and barely ever thinking about my ex, it still felt like I had finally put this part of my life behind me.

Best of all, whenever I was tempted to think about my ex or feel guilty or sad or angry about my breakup, those negative emotions felt strangely played out and unnecessary. Honestly, after I wrote my letter, thinking about my breakup at all felt terribly boring. It was like I was hearing the same story for the hundredth time. I was simply over it. This letter had become my last word on the subject. I had said everything I wanted to say, felt everything I needed to feel, and after that, I had brushed my hands off and put the whole thing aside. I was done.

Shortly after going through a breakup, many people continue talking to their exes in hopes of finding closure. They think their ex will say or do something that will provide some sort of instant relief. Unfortunately, closure isn't something your ex can give you. It's something you have to give yourself. You have to move past this relationship. You have to understand that it's over. Your ex can't do these things for you. By writing this letter, you'll give yourself the closure you've been looking for. Instead of wondering if you're over your ex, you'll have it in writing. Instead of leaving things open-ended forever, you'll have proof on paper that it's finished. You'll give yourself the closure no one else could, and after you tear that letter up and toss it aside, you won't have a reason to revisit this breakup ever again – unless it's to remind yourself of just how far you've come.

CHAPTER 6
- Looking Ahead -

And just like that, we've reached the last stop on this magic carpet ride. I understand that no book can take all of your pain away instantly, even if the pages are laced with morphine, but I truly hope you're feeling more motivated, more excited about your future, and more hopeful than you were 23,000 words ago. Remember, you have the tools. You have the techniques. You know what to do, and what to strive for. To be honest, this breakup doesn't stand a chance against you now. Stay focused, use what you've learned, and soon you'll be feeling in top shape. You'll be back to your old self. And this breakup will be nothing but a reminder that you can rise to any challenge. Before we close up shop though, and I send you on your soon-to-be-completely-recovered way, I wanted to cover two more important topics that you'll deal with in the months and years ahead: fear and forgiveness. These are the two big F-words that'll play a big role in all of your future relationships, so I think they're worth talking about here.

To start, let's focus on forgiveness. Of course, I'm sure you already know that forgiveness is important. You've watched enough movies, heard enough stories, and seen enough inspirational quotes to know that forgiveness is good for the soul. But when it comes to breakups, it can be hard to forgive an ex. Damn hard. Sure, there's a chance your ex might have ended things with compassion, grace and understanding, and in that case, forgiveness will come a lot easier. But there's also a good chance that things were far more difficult for you.

Instead of kindness, you might have only faced contempt. Instead of compassion, there might have only been hostility. You might have been insulted or ridiculed or even had to deal with cheating. And if that's the case, forgiveness is probably the last thing you want to think about right now.

And that's okay.

Forgiveness is a long road that you don't have to walk down right this second, but there's a reason I wanted to bring it up now. To put it simply, forgiveness is good for you. Studies tell us that people who forgive are healthier and happier than people who hold on to grudges.[26] Most importantly, forgiving your ex will actually strengthen and improve all of your future relationships. After all, if you're unable to forgive your ex, or unwilling to even try, the pain from your breakup is going to be fresh in your memory. Your anger is going to have a VIP pass to your thought patterns, and when you find yourself in a new relationship, all of those negative feelings will be front and center in your mind, making you more distant, more defensive, and less likely to enjoy everything your new relationship has to offer. And you don't want that to happen. If you found a great new relationship, wouldn't it be a shame to let an old, tired relationship get in the way? Wouldn't it be ridiculous to let the wrong woman come between you and the right woman? This is why forgiveness is so important. By letting go of your anger and resentment, you can move forward in your life without a lick of emotional baggage in tow. You can start a new relationship off on the right foot, without the past interfering in the slightest.

And yet, I know it's tough. I've been through it.

Forgiveness in a lot of ways feels like admitting defeat. It feels like she wins, and you lose. She was right, and you were wrong. But that's not how forgiveness really works. Letting go of your anger doesn't change what happened. It can't rewrite history. It doesn't excuse or justify what your ex did either. You are not conceding that she was right all along or that you deserved what happened. At the same time, it doesn't devalue what you went through, or mean that you were overreacting to the situation.

After my divorce, I held on to my anger for a long time. I felt like I had to. The worse my ex was to me, the angrier I needed to be with her. I had to balance out the pain, but in the end, the only person my anger was affecting was me. It wasn't helping me in any way. It was only slowing me down. When I decided to forgive my ex, it wasn't for her sake, it was for mine. I deserved to be free of resentment and anger, and that's what forgiveness is all about. It doesn't change the past. It doesn't wash away how your ex handled things. It only changes how you feel for the better. After all, if you were given a choice between being angry, bitter and resentful, or being happy, peaceful and content, what would you choose? And really, you do have a say in the matter. You can hold on to that anger for years. Or you can try to let it go, and let it be replaced by much better things.

Besides your ex, there's one more person who deserves a little forgiveness around here – you. No doubt, you made a few mistakes in your relationship. We all do. No one's ever played a perfect game when it comes to romance. And that's just a part of life. Instead of feeling terrible about your mistakes, however, I want you to try something completely different: I want you to cherish your mistakes. Because without them, how could you get any better? How could you improve without first facing your flaws? You may not realize it right now, but mistakes are the building blocks of greatness. They will guide you, push you, and help you along the way. They will teach you things you might never have known and give you a wealth of new experience to draw from. But here's the catch – it's up to you to reflect on them, learn from them, and try your best to not repeat them. Use those mistakes for all they're worth, but don't keep beating yourself up over them. Guilt is a great tool to help remind you of what you did and how to do better in the future, but the key is to not overdo it. With the relationship gone and the pain you've felt, you've already paid a high price, and being angry at yourself isn't going to help in any way. It's not going to fix what happened. It's not going to change anything. As long as you've owned up to your mistakes, learned everything you can from them, and committed yourself to not repeating them, what else can you do?

This isn't to say you shouldn't feel bad when you do bad things, but let's keep things in perspective. You didn't rob a bank. You didn't kick an orphan. You simply made a few errors in judgment, which may or may not have brought about the end of your relationship. But that's what learning and growing is all about. Life is a learning process. And even though some lessons take a heavy toil, rest assured that you're now better equipped to have a healthier and happier relationship in the future. Until then, try to forgive yourself. You know how much you've gone through. You know how much you wish you could change things. Chances are you've paid enough already, and now's not the time to work against yourself. Now's the time to start building yourself back up.

That covers the small, medium, and super-sized mistakes, but I know a lot of guys get hung up on the tiniest of foibles. I remember reading a post from a guy who forgot to do the dishes one day, and when his girlfriend came home and saw the mess, she broke up with him on the spot. Weeks later, he still couldn't get over the feeling that they would still be together if he had only washed a few spoons. He knew it was absurd. Everyone reading knew it was absurd, but he couldn't help feeling angry at himself, and unfortunately, I know exactly where he's coming from. I spent many nights wondering if I could have saved my relationship if only I had said this instead of that or did one thing instead of another. I was disappointed and angry with myself, but even if I did things a little differently, would it really have mattered? If that guy had done the dishes, would he still be in a relationship? Probably not.

At the end of the day, the ultimate goal of dating is to find someone who will stand by you through better or worse, through thick and thin, in sickness and in health. It's to find someone who will love you unconditionally. It's to build a relationship that can flourish during the good times and still stay strong during the worst of times. The right relationship, in theory, should be able to work through the worst of the worst situations. With that in mind, if that guy's relationship couldn't survive a few dirty dishes, what would happen if he lost his job or ended up in the hospital? Isn't it better that his relationship ended then, instead of when he really needed it? The same is true for you. If you're worried about the little mistakes you made, don't waste your time. Maybe you could have done things differently, but in the end, it probably wouldn't have changed anything at all. If your relationship wasn't strong enough to survive the problems it had or the mistakes you made, if it wasn't going to last through thick and thin, then it simply wasn't the right relationship for you. It wasn't the one you've been looking for – the one that will support you when you need it the most. And even though that's a tough pill to choke down, trust me, it's much better to find this all out now than in five or ten years down the line. This breakup has saved you valuable time. From here on out, you don't have to spend another minute in the wrong relationship. Instead, you're now free to go out there and find the right one.

Just to be crystal clear here, please don't use this as an excuse to do whatever you want to a future girlfriend, of course. Don't spend Christmas dinner slapping her sister on the ass and yelling, "With the power of unconditional love I can do anything!" You still have to work at every relationship. You still have to give it your all. You still have to strive to make your partner happy. This is simply a reminder to not sweat the little stuff. Don't lose sleep wondering if you could have saved your relationship. Even though every tiny mistake might seem like a huge deal right now, in reality, they mattered far less than you think.

Forgiveness might seem like a big hurdle, but fear is a whole 'nother beast entirely. When you think of fear, the first thing that probably comes to mind is scary movies or skydiving or going to work after a three-day weekend, but fear actually plays a tremendous role in your romantic endeavors as well. And not in a good way. In fact, fear is the single, biggest obstacle we all face in our search for romantic happiness. Bar none. When we want to ask someone out, fear will chime in and tell us that she'll say no. On a first date, fear will whisper that it's not going well, even if it is. When we're in a good relationship, fear will advise us to be jealous or distance. It will tell us that relationships never last. After a breakup, fear will sit us down, look us in the eye, and impolitely state that we're probably going to be alone forever.

At the beginning, middle and end of our relationships, fear is there to lead us astray and stop us from ever finding happiness. Unfortunately, it's easy to believe everything it tells us. Fear has been keeping us safe since we were kids. It's kept us from putting our hands in fires, touching electrical outlets, eating bugs, or playing in traffic. It's done its job for a long, long time, but when it comes to romance, it simply can't help us in the same way. And how could it? When it comes to relationships, fear wants the worst for you. It wants you to stay distant, never open up, be jealous and controlling and suspicious, be pessimistic, never try anything new, never have hope, and preferably, never ask a woman out in the first place. Fear doesn't care about how great the reward is. It only cares about the risk. But sometimes a little pain is worth the prize. You can't have a great relationship, after all, if you're constantly worried that it's going to end. You can't grow close to someone, if you're too scared to trust them. You can't even start a relationship, if you're too afraid to make the first move. You don't want to miss out on an amazing part of life just because fear told you to. You don't want to look back on life and say you never took a chance. Luckily, fear doesn't call the shots around here. You do.

When fear starts mouthing off in the future, you alone get to decide if you're going follow its advice or if you're going to grit your teeth and power through it. The choice is yours. Courage, after all, isn't about having no fear at all. It's about going after what you really want and telling fear to get the hell out of your way. As the months and years pass by, make a promise with yourself: never run from your fears. Instead, make your fears run from you. If there's a girl you want to ask out one day, go for it. Do it. Remember, fear will always, always tell you no, but that girl in question might just tell you yes. You have an infinitely better chance by asking her out, than you do by simply walking away. Could she possibly say no? Of course, but in the grand scheme of things, would it matter?

As I've said before, everyone has different preferences. Some women like guys who are covered in tattoos. Some women like clean-cut guys who look good in suits. If you go up to a woman who's only interested in dating lumberjacks, and you're not wearing a single piece of flannel, those are just the breaks. It's not your fault. It's nothing to worry about. She's simply not the right one for you, and best of all, now you know. That's one less woman you have to wonder about or pine over. By scratching her off your list, you've actually narrowed the playing field and increased your chances of finding someone special. In truth, every wrong woman you meet and get involved with will only get you closer and closer to finding the right one. Over time, you'll learn. You'll grow. You'll figure out what you really want in a partner and in a relationship. And one day, when you finally meet the right girl and walk away hand-in-hand, you won't be thinking about that lumberjack-fetishist who turned you down because you didn't smell like cedar chips. You'll be thinking about the girl by your side, and you'll know that it was all worth it.

Of course, even when you're in a great relationship, fear's going to be there telling you that it's not going to last. It's going to remind you of everything you went through during this breakup and make you think that it's going to happen all over again. But remember, you aren't like every other guy out there. Your ex isn't like every other girl. The next woman you meet isn't going to be exactly like your ex. Even if you ended up dating her identical twin sister, which would be really awkward during the holidays, your relationship would still end up being completely different. That's because no two people, or relationships, are exactly alike. You can't judge every woman out there based on your ex. You can't judge all of your future relationships based on this past one. That wouldn't be fair to you or to the other three billion women on this planet. When you do meet someone new, she might be the right one, or she might not. But don't let fear decide for you. When it comes to romance, fear is always an option, but it's never the answer. When it tries to make you doubt yourself or your relationship, when it pushes you to be jealous or controlling, remind yourself, fear is not there to help you. It won't better your relationship, or your life. It won't make you happy. It won't make you content. So don't let it stop you from going after what you really want.

To finish things up, you know you have to face your fears, and now is as good as time as any. In fact, fear is already taking a huge toll on you. It's one of the main reasons this breakup hurts as much as it does. But what if you had absolutely no fear about the future? What if you knew for a <u>fact</u> that everything was going to work out for the best, that you were going to end up far happier than you were before, and that you'd find someone you're even more compatible with? Would you still feel as bad as you do now right not? Absolutely not.

Of course, I can't guarantee all of those things are going to happen, but there's a damn good chance they will. You are in control now. You can make anything happen. Fear wants you to believe that your best times are behind you, that you're never going to be as happy again, but that's anything but the case. You and I both ended up on a different path than we originally planned. Sure, it might be a little steeper. It might be a little rockier. But it also might end up being far better than the one you were on. It was for me, and with everything you know now, there's a good chance it will be for you too. This breakup isn't the end of your story. It's only the beginning, and now's the time to start writing the next great chapter.

With that said, go ahead, throw on some music, start planning some weekly goals, and jot down a few lines in your grateful journal. A few months from now, start working on your foundations and go from there. You've got plenty to keep you busy and plenty to look forward to. To put it simply, you've got this. Don't let fear stand in your way. Stay focused. Stay driven. Be good to yourself. Be good to the people around you. Finally, I want to thank you for reading, and I want to wish you the best of luck. Now, get out there, put this book to work, and go show this breakup who's boss.

One last thing…

I've read the statistics, and it turns out nearly 4.6 million books are published every second on Amazon.com (give or take). Suffice it to say, in the grand scheme of things, this book is pretty difficult to find. Especially since I'm a first-time author. That is why, if you liked what you read and think it could help other people in the future, please consider leaving a short review on Amazon. Just a few words from you can make this book much easier to find for everyone else. I would truly appreciate it. Thanks again and best of luck...

- Nick

REFERENCES

1 Paul, P. (2010, July 24). A Young Man's Lament: Love Hurts! http://www.nytimes.com/2010/07/25/fashion/25Studied.html

2 Fisher, H., Brown, L., Aron, A., Strong, G., & Mashek, D. (n.d.). Reward, Addiction, and Emotion Regulation Systems Associated With Rejection in Love. Journal of Neurophysiology, 51-60.

3 Bernatzky, G., Presch, M., Anderson, M., & Panksepp, J. (n.d.). Emotional Foundations Of Music As A Non-pharmacological Pain Management Tool In Modern Medicine. Neuroscience & Biobehavioral Reviews, 1989-1999.

4 Nauert, R. (n.d.). Music Soothes Anxiety, Reduces Pain. Retrieved from http://psychcentral.com/news/2011/12/23/music-soothes-anxiety-reduces-pain/32952.html

5 Bernatzky, G., Presch, M., Anderson, M., & Panksepp, J. (n.d.). Emotional Foundations Of Music As A Non-pharmacological Pain Management Tool In Modern Medicine. Neuroscience & Biobehavioral Reviews, 1989-1999.

6 Salimpoor, V., Benovoy, M., Larcher, K., Dagher, A., & Zatorre, R. (n.d.). Anatomically distinct dopamine release during anticipation and experience of peak emotion to music. Nature Neuroscience, 257-262.

7 Vennum, A. (n.d.). Passion pitfall: Research finds that rekindling a romance often extinguishes a couple's happiness. Feb. 20, 2012. K-state.edu

8 Exercise treatment for depression: Efficacy and dose response
Andrea L. Dunn, Madhukar H. Trivedi, James B. Kampert, Camillia G. Clark, Heather O. Chambliss

[9] Avnet, L. (2013, March 27). 13 Mental Health Benefits Of Exercise. Retrieved from http://www.huffingtonpost.com/2013/03/27/mental-health-benefits-exercise_n_2956099.html

[10] Kraft, T., & Pressman, S. (n.d.). Grin and Bear It: The Influence of Manipulated Facial Expression on the Stress Response.*Psychological Science,* 1372-1378.

[11] 'I Can't Believe She Did That To Me...' (n.d.). Retrieved November 26, 2014, from http://www.huffingtonpost.co.uk/2011/12/22/justin-timberlake-britney-spears-cry-me-a-river_n_1164520.html

[12] Cacioppo, J., Cacioppo, S., Gonzaga, G., Ogburn, E., & Vanderweele, T. (n.d.). Marital satisfaction and break-ups differ across on-line and off-line meeting venues.*Proceedings of the National Academy of Sciences,* 10135-10140.

[13] Keng, C. (n.d.). Employees Who Stay In Companies Longer Than Two Years Get Paid 50% Less. Retrieved from http://www.forbes.com/sites/cameronkeng/2014/06/22/employees-that-stay-in-companies-longer-than-2-years-get-paid-50-less/

[14] Harter, S. (1999) *The construction of the self*. New York: Guilford.

[15] The Top 20 Traits Women Want in a Man. (n.d.). Retrieved from http://www.menshealth.com/mhlists/most_desirable_traits/Top_5_Physical_Attributes.php

[16] Staff, M. (2014, February 5). Fitness. Retrieved from http://www.mayoclinic.com/health/exercise/HQ01676

[17] Valeo, T. (n.d.). Health Benefits of Good Friends. Retrieved from http://www.webmd.com/balance/features/good-friends-are-good-for-you

[18] Achor, S. (2010). *The happiness advantage: the seven principles of positive psychology that fuel success and performance at work*. New York: Broadway Books.

[19] http://www.nydailynews.com/entertainment/tv-movies/americans-spend-34-hours-week-watching-tv-nielsen-numbers-article-1.1162285

[20] Wood, W., Quinn, J.M., & Kashy, D. (2002). *Habits in everyday life: Thought, emotion, and action*. Journal of Personality and Social Psychology, 83, 1281–1297.

[21] Duhigg, C. (2012). *The power of habit: why we do what we do in life and business*. New York: Random House.

[22] Knox D, Zusman M, Kaluzny M, Cooper C. College student recovery from a broken heart. *College Student Journal* [serial online]. September 2000;34(3):322-324.

[23] Carney, D. R., Cuddy, A. J. C., & Yap, A. J. (2010). Power posing: Brief nonverbal displays affect neuroendocrine levels and risk tolerance. *Psychological Science, 21 (10)*, 1363–1368.

[24] Maslow, A. H.. "A Theory Of Human Motivation." *Psychological Review*: 370-396. Print.

[25] Baikie, K. A.. "Emotional And Physical Health Benefits Of Expressive Writing." *Advances in Psychiatric Treatment*: 338-346. Print.

[26] Van Oyen, C. Witvilet, T.E. Ludwig and K. L. Vander Lann, "Granting Forgiveness or Harboring Grudges: Implications for Emotions, Physiology and Health," Psychological Science no. 12 (2001):117-23

Printed in Poland
by Amazon Fulfillment
Poland Sp. z o.o., Wrocław

36878743R00056